Preaching the
Four Gospels
with
Confidence

The Preacher's Toolbox

Prophetic Preaching

Inspirational Preaching

Interpretation and Application

Sermon Preparation

Preaching the Four Gospels with Confidence

Preaching the Hard Words of Jesus

Preaching the Four Gospels with Confidence

Steven D. Mathewson

Craig Brian Larson, General Editor

HENDRICKSON
PUBLISHERS

Preaching the Four Gospels with Confidence

Hendrickson Publishers Marketing, LLC
P. O. Box 3473
Peabody, Massachusetts 01961-3473

ISBN 978-1-59856-702-1

Printed in the United States of America

First Hendrickson Edition Printing — July 2013

Library of Congress Cataloging-in-Publication Data

Mathewson, Steven D. (Steven Dale), 1961–
   Preaching the four gospels with confidence / Steven D. Mathewson.
       pages cm. — (The preacher's toolbox ; Book 5)
       ISBN 978-1-59856-702-1 (alk. paper)
       1. Bible. Gospels—Homiletical use. 2. Preaching. I. Title.
   BS2555.54.M38 2013
   251—dc23
                           2013002405

Dedication

To Haddon Robinson,
a mentor and friend
whose godliness, preaching, teaching, and confidence in me
has impacted me to an extent I am unable to measure.
Haddon, I thank God every time I remember you!

CONTENTS

ACKNOWLEDGMENTS

More than fifty years ago, George Ladd suggested that Matthew 24:14 is the most important single verse in the Word of God for God's people today. This verse contains Jesus' words: "And this gospel of the kingdom will be preached in the whole world as a testimony to all nations, and then the end will come." What a privilege to write a couple of volumes which will, I pray, help pastors proclaim the gospel of the kingdom from the four Gospels.

First and foremost, I thank Brian Larson for inviting me to partner with PreachingToday.com and Hendrickson Publishers to help pastors overcome the challenges they face when preaching the four Gospels. Along the way, this project turned into *two* volumes! I am grateful for Brian's vision, support, and encouragement. It has been tremendous in every respect.

I am grateful to the gospels scholars who were willing to take time out of their busy schedules to help me think through many of the issues discussed in these volumes. I appreciate the breakfast and lunch meetings I had with Grant Osborne and Craig Blomberg. David Turner graciously took the time to interact with me extensively by e-mail on matters of Second Temple Judaism—the context in which the events in the four Gospels took place. D. A. Carson has kindly taken time over the past six years to meet me for breakfast and allow me to pick his brain on a variety of exegetical, theological, and pastoral issues. His love for the gospel inspires me.

The elders of the Evangelical Free Church of Libertyville (IL) have been very supportive of my writing ministry and have encouraged me to serve the wider church through it. Their influence has made me a better pastor and preacher. So I offer my thanks to Bryan Cope, Tom Erickson, Joe Giovanetto, Jim Gruenewald, Curt Gustafson, Jerry Parker, Todd Ronne, and Chris Walter. I also want to single out Rick Chalupnik, our church's pastor of adult ministries, for the insights he offers week after week as we think through what our church family needs to hear from the sermon text for the following Sunday.

How can I fail to thank my dear friend Dave Goetz for the influence he has had on my life, ministry, and writing. He is truly a friend who sticks closer than a brother (Prov. 18:24). Dave is the first editor to give me a shot at writing for publication.

Finally, I am deeply grateful to my wife, Priscilla, who understands the value of the writing ministry God has given me and who encourages me to carve out the time it requires. I love her more than words can say.

Above all, I give thanks for the grace God has given me "through the appearing of our Savior, Christ Jesus, who has destroyed death and has brought life and immortality to light through the gospel" (2 Tim. 1:10). What an incredible privilege to serve as a herald of his gospel. To him be glory and honor forever and ever.

INTRODUCTION

The people to whom we preach week after week resemble Émile Cailliet.[1] Émile Cailliet was a young soldier in the French army during World War I. A university graduate, he had never seen a Bible and was an agnostic. But the inadequacy of his worldview overwhelmed him during his military service. He began questioning the usefulness of the philosophical ideas he had learned in college. What use is it, he asked, "when your own buddy—at the time speaking to you of his mother—dies standing in front of you, a bullet in his chest?"

Then a bullet struck Cailliet as well, and he spent nine months recovering in a hospital. After his release from the hospital and his discharge from the French army, he resumed his graduate studies. But something had happened to Cailliet. He writes: "I had returned to my books, but they were no longer the same books. Neither was my motivation the same motivation. Reading in literature and philosophy, I found myself probing in depth for meaning. During long night watches in the foxholes, I had in a strange way been longing—I must say it, however queer it may sound—for a book that would understand me."

Since Cailliet knew of no such book, he decided to write one for himself. Whenever he read a passage from a book that spoke to his condition, he would copy it in a leather-bound pocket-sized book. The day came when he put the finishing touches on his book. It was a bright, sunny day, but as he sat under a tree in a garden and read over his little book, his joy at his accomplishment was clouded by disappointment. Instead of speaking to his condition, the passages simply reminded him of the circumstances in which he had chosen them.

Cailliet recalls: "Then I knew that the whole undertaking would not work, simply because it was of my own making. It carried no strength of persuasion. In a dejected mood, I put the little book back in my pocket."

At that very moment, his wife appeared at the gate of the garden, pushing a baby carriage. She was carrying a Bible given to her by a pastor she had met on her walk. Émile, who at age twenty-three had never seen a Bible, asked for it, grabbed it, and rushed to his study to read it. He opened it to the Gospels and began to read deep into the night. Cailliet describes what happened as he read the Gospels: "All of a sudden, the realization dawned upon me: This was 'the book that would understand me.' . . . And lo and behold, as I looked through them [the Gospels], the One of whom they spoke, the One who spoke and acted in them became alive to me. . . . While it seemed absurd to speak of a book understanding a man, this could be said of the Bible." At last, in the Gospels, Émile Cailliet found the story that understood him.[2]

Whenever we preach the Gospels and present the story of the One who speaks and acts in them, we proclaim to our listeners the only story that understands them. What a high and noble privilege to preach the Gospels of Matthew, Mark, Luke, and John!

This book is for preachers who love the gospel and want to preach it well from the four Gospels—Matthew, Mark, Luke, and John. Good preaching of the gospel from the Gospels requires preachers who take great pains to understand the Gospels truly and explain them clearly.[3]

This latter point seems like a "given." What better place to preach the gospel than from the four Gospels themselves? Yet pastors run into obstacles when they set out to preach the gospel accounts of Matthew, Mark, Luke, and John. The editors at PreachingToday.com spent several months identifying the most pressing challenges preachers face when preaching the four Gospels. They listened to preachers and reflected on the challenges they face in their own preaching. Later in the discussion, they brought me on board and invited me to write a couple of books on the matter. So I added to their initial list of challenges based on my own frustrations in preaching the Gospels. Then I queried colleagues in my denomination and in my pastoral networks. This led to more refinement and finally to a list of sixteen challenges we must overcome in preaching the Gospels.

This volume will tackle the first seven challenges we identified. A sequel, *Preaching the Hard Words of Jesus*, will zero in on the words of Jesus. But before we narrow our focus specifically to what Jesus said, there are some general challenges we must overcome.

In chapter 1, "Right Sizing," we address the challenge of how we decide the length of a preaching unit. The length of the Gospels themselves seems to require larger preaching units than we might choose when preaching through an Epistle. Do we sacrifice breadth for depth, or depth for breadth? Furthermore, narrative accounts take a while to unfold. Splitting a long narrative into two or three sermons may not be feasible since the meaning of the narrative will not unfold until it is resolved.

Chapter 2, "Are Jesus and Paul on the Same Page?" faces the challenge of the relationship between the Gospels and the rest of the New Testament—Acts and the Epistles. Increasingly, readers of the New Testament are pitting Jesus versus Paul. After all, the emphases of Jesus and the apostles who wrote the New Testament seem a bit different. How are we to reconcile the theology of the Gospels with the theology of the rest of the New Testament?

Chapter 3, "Background Check," works with the challenge of properly using the Jewish and Greco-Roman background of the Gospels. One popular preacher claims that when Jesus called Peter, Andrew, James, and John, he "took some boys who didn't make the cut and changed the course of human history."[4] But where do the Gospels say these fishermen called by Jesus didn't make the cut? According to this preacher, the fact that Jesus called fishermen to follow him shows these early followers had not advanced from the *Bet Talmud* phase of learning to the *Bet Midrash* level where the brightest students advanced. That will preach! But should it be preached? Do the Jewish sources that explain the *Bet Talmud* and *Bet Midrash* phases really apply to the time of Jesus?

In chapter 4, "Conflicting Reports?" we address the challenge that surfaces when we compare parallel accounts. For example, the Synoptic Gospels all report that the transfiguration took place after Jesus' stunning prediction that some of his disciples would not die before they saw the kingdom of God. Both Matthew and Mark report that the transfiguration happened six days after this statement (Matt. 17:1; Mark 9:2). However, Luke 9:28 reports that Jesus said this "about eight days" later. There's nothing wrong with Luke estimating here, but it seems odd in light of his meticulous research (see Luke 1:1–4) and the reality that he would have had access to Mark's Gospel and Matthew's Gospel when he wrote his account. His estimation, then, seems almost deliberate. How are we to understand places like this where parallel accounts seem to contradict each other?

Chapter 5, "Dealing with Darkness," meets the challenge of Jesus' interactions with Satan and demons. What do we do with a story in which Jesus shows his power over a legion of demons by casting them out of a man who lived among the tombs and sending this legion into a herd of pigs that plunges off a cliff to their death in the Sea of Galilee (Luke 8:26–38)? Have we failed to show how Jesus' encounters with demons are normative for believers today in the struggles that the apostle Paul claims go beyond flesh and blood and extend to evil spiritual forces (Eph. 6:12)? In what sense are Jesus' encounters with Satan and demons normative for today?

Chapter 6, "On Purpose," takes on the challenge we face in aligning our application of what Jesus does and says with the gospel writer's intent. We know that Jesus wants us to follow his example in serving others (see Matt. 20:28; Mark 10:45), but how far can we go in following Jesus as our example? Should we expect ourselves and other Christ-followers to heal the sick, raise the dead, and shut down sea storms? What about his instructions to the seventy-two in Luke 10:4 not to take a purse or bag or sandals on their short-term mission trip? How do we apply that to our situations today, especially since Jesus modified those instructions in Luke 22:36?

Finally, in chapter 7, "Against Counterfeits," we meet the challenge that comes with affirming the authority of the four Gospels in a time when the "lost gospels" are gaining popularity.

Dan Brown's novel *The Da Vinci Code* simply popularized a sentiment that has been brewing for the past decade or so in the writings of Elaine Pagels and Bart Ehrman. How do we help listeners realize the claim is patently false that "more than *eighty* gospels were considered for the New Testament, and yet only a relative few were chosen for inclusion"?[5] How do we respond to the young university graduate who asks how we can be sure that Jesus is really the Son of God when the marginal note at the bottom of the page tells him that some manuscripts do not have the words *the Son of God* in Mark 1:1?

Let me encourage you to "take up and read" this book as a way of helping you negotiate the challenges you must overcome when preaching the Gospels to your late-modern listeners. You will benefit either by reading the chapters in the order they appear or by skipping around to the chapters that deal with the challenges that are most pressing for you and your listeners. Then check out the sequel, *Preaching the Hard Words of Jesus,* to get help with preaching the words of Jesus himself.

Deepening Your Love for the Gospel and the Four Gospels

My prayer is that this book will deepen your love for the gospel of Jesus Christ and for the four Gospels that proclaim the story of Jesus' birth, baptism, temptation, ministry, teaching, death, and resurrection. I pray that your preaching of the gospel in the four Gospels will capture your imagination and the imaginations of your listeners, drawing you and them into a deeper love for Jesus.

Both nonbelievers and believers need to hear the story. For people who say "they like Jesus but not the church," preaching the story of Jesus from the four Gospels may be the best way to introduce them to the gospel.[6] Even those who have been believers for decades and think they know the story of Jesus and his love need to hear a fresh preaching of it. When pastors faithfully expose the ideas communicated by the Evangelists, as well as by the Savior whose words they record, veteran believers will rediscover the freshness of the gospel as well as "the Jesus they never knew."[7]

1

RIGHT SIZING

Determining the optimum length of
sermon series and preaching units

I love the comment at the very end of John's Gospel: "Jesus did many other things as well. If every one of them were written down, I suppose that even the whole world would not have room for the books that would be written" (21:25). That's how magnificent Jesus is!

But frankly, I struggle to proclaim all the things Jesus did that *are* written down. So many texts, so little time. This struggle creeps into a couple of key challenges I face in any literary genre of Scripture but particularly in the Gospels. They have to do with the length of a sermon series and with the length of the preaching units within those series.

I recently shared with several pastors a proposed plan for preaching through Luke. The size of the preaching units was generous, yet the plan still required sixty-seven sermons. My plan called for preaching the birth narratives of Luke 1–2 during the Advent or Christmas season at the end of a calendar year. Then preaching through Luke 3–18 occupied all but five Sundays of the next year. The plan called for continuing with Luke 19 at the beginning of year three and wrapping up the series with a message on Luke 24 on Easter. I thought it was a great plan, but my pastoral colleagues questioned whether my congregation could take such a long series without a break.

Gifted preachers like John Piper and Mark Driscoll may be able to sustain people's interest in the same book of Scripture for more than a year or two, but most congregations and pastors need the variety that is built into Scripture itself. So how long should my series be? If it is on the long side, how do I keep people engaged? I have met people who claim to dislike the Gospels of Matthew, Mark, Luke, or John. When I probe this a bit, I find that a previous pastor spent months or years in one of those books. The length of his sermon series simply exceeded the length of their tolerance. These are people who love the Scriptures, but they grasped intuitively that a gospel is to be read through in two hours, not two years.

A related challenge is the size of preaching units. Should I preach all three "lost" stories in Luke 15 together, or should I combine the first two shorter stories and preach a single sermon on the longer story of the lost son? Recently, while preaching through John, I decided to preach through all seventy-one verses of chapter 6 in one sermon. Gulp! I did that because I thought the development of Jesus' argument and the choice it forces hearers to make (vv. 60–71) was so compelling that I needed to work through the whole chapter in one sermon. How, then, can I cover adequately a passage that takes more than five minutes just to read?

I have six theses about the length of sermon series and preaching units. (I wanted to find a seventh so I would have a perfect number, but, alas, I could not.) I have deliberately identified these as theses rather than elements of a formula, because your preaching context is different from mine and different from the church in the next town. Even within your ministry, the particular needs and questions will change over time. People always need to hear what Jesus said and did, but what is going on within your zip code will dictate how you approach questions related to length of series or length of text. Here, then, are my six theses.

1. People need to know the story of Jesus, and accomplishing this will require longer series and blocks of text.

Both believers and nonbelievers are fascinated with Jesus. But a decline in biblical literacy and the renewed interest in revisionist accounts of Jesus' life and teaching have created a hazy, shallow understanding of Jesus—who he is, what he did, and what he said. As one pastor observed about the university students he queried about Jesus, "They like Jesus but not the church."[1]

This sentiment stems in part from the disconnect between the way Jesus lived and the way Jesus' church behaves,[2] but it also results from people's ignorance of the Gospels. People hear snippets about the biblical Jesus and overlay their picture of him with images of a shaman or guru imported from Eastern religions like Buddhism or Hinduism. Or they hear Elaine Pagels or Bart Ehrman tout the "lost gospels" and imagine Jesus as a boy who used his power to lengthen a board that his earthly father, Joseph, cut too short while building a custom bed.[3]

More than ever, our generation needs to hear the Gospels preached from beginning to end so they can know the true story of Jesus—who he is, what he did, and what he said. This will require some longer series. Mark's Gospel consists of sixteen chapters, but the other three top out at twenty-plus chapters. It will definitely take more sermons to preach through Matthew than Philippians or Malachi!

The need for listeners to grasp the story of Jesus will require preaching through longer texts for each sermon. This is a function of narrative. Preachers can afford to work with preaching units of six to twelve verses in the Epistles, but in the Gospels we may need to preach thirty verses to cover a whole narrative—a story whose plot has been resolved.

Without a good grasp of how the larger story of Jesus develops, listeners will not be able to see how the various parables, pronouncements, miracles, and gracious acts of Jesus fit together.

2. A good way to keep a series from being too long is to break it into a miniseries.

After accepting a pastorate in the north suburbs of Chicago, I decided to begin my preaching ministry there by working through John. I wanted to lay the right groundwork, building my ministry on the gospel of Jesus Christ. In addition, because *The Da Vinci Code* movie was due for release in a couple of weeks, I wanted to address the challenges it threw at the true picture of Jesus. But for various reasons I did not want to spend six months in a row on John—the time it would take me as I had divided the book into twenty-four preaching units.

Divisions for John's Gospel

Rather than preach straight through John, therefore, I used its natural divisions to create two series. First, I preached a thirteen-week series, titled The Jesus You Need to Know, from John 1–12. Then I took a three-month hiatus to preach another series before returning to finish John. My second series lasted eleven weeks, covered John 13–21, and was titled Jesus' Mission in High Definition.

Even if I had preached straight through John, I still would have divided the book into two distinct series. John 1–12 is commonly identified as the Book of Signs, since "Jesus is at work in public . . . showing signs and teaching to diverse public audiences."[4] John 13–21 is commonly identified as the Book of Glory, since Jesus' elevation to glory on the cross is imminent. This latter half of John contains Jesus' farewell instructions given privately to his followers (John 13–17) and then ends with a detailed account of Jesus' passion and resurrection (John 18–21).[5]

Divisions for Matthew's Gospel

For Matthew, some scholars have taken the alternation between narrative and discourse as the key to the book's structure. Between the birth narratives at the beginning (Matt. 1–2) and the passion and resurrection narratives at the end (Matt. 26–28), there are five sections that each begin with narrative and end with a discourse. As David Turner notes, "Matthew marks each of the five transitions from discourse back to narrative with the phrase . . . 'when Jesus had finished'; 7:28; 11:1; 13:53; 19:1; 26:1."[6] This leads to the following structure:[7]

I. Introduction: the origin of Jesus the Messiah (1–2)

II. The gospel of the kingdom (3–7)

    A. Narrative (3–4)

    B. Discourse: Sermon on the Mount (5–7)

III. The kingdom expands (8–10)

    A. Narrative (8–9)

    B. Discourse (10)

IV. Opposition to the kingdom increases (11–13)

    A. Narrative (11–12)

    B. Discourse (13)

V. Opposition to the kingdom intensifies (14–18)

    A. Narrative (14–17)

    B. Discourse (18)

VI. Opposition leads to warning and a call for readiness (19–25)

    A. Narrative (19–23)

    B. Discourse (24–25)

VII. Epilogue: The passion, resurrection, and commission of Jesus the Messiah (26–28)

Working with this rough outline, you could break Matthew into seven miniseries if preaching straight through the book. Or, if you planned for some time gaps between the sermon series, going with two or three series makes the most sense. Otherwise listeners would lose a sense of continuity. A two-part series might consist of preaching through chapters 1–13 and then later through chapters 14–28. For a three-part series, you could divide Matthew into chapters 1–10, 11–18, and 19–28.

There is another way to break Matthew into a three-part series. Some scholars have noted the expression "from that time on Jesus began" in Matthew 4:17 and 16:21 as a key indicator of structure.[8] Craig Blomberg proposes this outline.[9]

I. Introduction to Jesus' ministry (1:1–4:16)

II. The development of Jesus' ministry (4:17–16:20)

III. The climax of Jesus' ministry (16:21–28:20).

For a two-part series using this approach, the breakdown consists of 1:1–16:20 and 16:21–28:20.

Divisions for Mark's Gospel

Mark's Gospel breaks into two or three natural divisions for pastors wanting to preach it in more than one sermon series. William Lane sees a key break between Mark 8:30 and 8:31, arguing that "with verse 31 an entirely new orientation is given to the Gospel."[10] The first major section of the Gospel ends with Peter's confession of Jesus as Messiah and Jesus' warning for his disciples not to tell anyone, while the second section begins the movement toward Jerusalem and opens with Jesus' first prediction of his death and resurrection.

More recently, R. T. France has proposed this breakdown into three acts.[11]

Act One: Galilee (1:14–8:21)

Act Two: On the way to Jerusalem (8:22–10:52)

Act Three: Jerusalem (11:1–16:8)

Divisions for Luke's Gospel

Luke lends itself to a two- or three-part sermon series. The best commentators agree on Luke's basic structure.[12]

I. Luke's preface and the birth and childhood of Jesus (1:1–2:52)

II. The preparation for Jesus' ministry (3:1–4:13)

III. Jesus' ministry in Galilee (4:14–9:50)

IV. Jesus' journey to Jerusalem (9:51–19:44)

V. Jesus in Jerusalem: his death and resurrection (19:45–24:53)

Working with this basic structure, a preacher could break the book into two series (1:1–9:50 and 9:51–24:53) or three series (1:1–9:50; 9:51–19:44; and 19:45–24:53). As I write this, I am currently preaching through Luke. I will divide it into three series, each separated by a three- to four-month break. But I will use one title for the entire series: Jesus and God's Plan for a Broken World. Each series will have a different feel to it. The first series will focus particularly on the identity of Jesus. The second will contain the bulk of his parables. The third will focus on the passion.

Whichever Gospel you preach, weigh the benefits of going straight through it versus giving your people a break between major chunks of it. If you preach it straight through, creating a different title for each major section can bring freshness and keep listeners from feeling stuck in the same book for months or years. On the other hand, if you break a Gospel down into two or three series and separate these by weeks or months, it might be wise to use the same title that holds the separate series together.

Timing is important. You might start Matthew or Luke during the Advent/Christmas season, that being a natural time to study Jesus' birth narratives. Then keep going when the calendar turns to January. Alternatively, you might time a series so that you preach the passion sections during the weeks leading up to Good Friday and Easter Sunday.

However you accomplish it, thinking in terms of multiple series can make it possible for you to preach through an entire Gospel and keep your listeners tracking with you.

3. Once your people know the story of Jesus, you should focus on key blocks of Jesus' teaching.

Throughout my ministry, I have alternated between preaching entire Gospels and preaching key blocks of Jesus' teaching.

I have taken congregations through the Sermon on the Mount (Matt. 5–7), the Parables of the Kingdom (Matt. 13), the Olivet Discourse (Matt. 24–25), and the Upper Room Discourse (John 13–17). I have also preached series on the parables of Jesus.

Another possibility would be a series titled The Hard Sayings of Jesus. Obvious candidates include John 6:25–28 (where Jesus invites his listeners to eat his flesh and drink his blood), Matthew 5:27–29 (where Jesus tells his followers to deal with lust by cutting off body parts), Luke 18:18–25 (where Jesus instructs the rich ruler to sell all his possessions), Luke 14:25–27 (where Jesus says his followers must hate their parents, spouses, and siblings), and Luke 16:9 (where Jesus counsels his followers to use worldly wealth to gain friends with the ultimate goal of being welcomed into eternal dwellings).

My mentor Haddon Robinson quips that these kinds of texts would be grist for a sermon series titled Things I Wish Jesus Had Not Said! The point is not to preach these texts because they are radical or disturbing. Rather, the radical or disturbing elements have a way of drawing our attention to critical concepts for those who follow Jesus and participate in God's kingdom. F. F. Bruce's book *The Hard Sayings of Jesus* provides useful leads and ideas.

A commitment to biblical theology may lead you to explore what Jesus says on particular topics such as wealth, marriage, faith, or obedience. The best way to do this is through the exposition of key parables or sayings on a given topic. You can pull together two or three or four texts on a given topic, or you could opt for a general series on What Jesus Says about Life's Big Issues.

Series that opt for a narrow slice of a particular Gospel or that organize themselves around a theme work best *after* listeners have gone through one or two Gospels and have a good grasp of the overall story.

4. Maintain the tension between breadth and depth when determining your preaching units.

For almost fifteen years, I lived ninety miles north of Yellowstone National Park. I referred to it affectionately as my family's backyard. When friends visited from out of state, I often took them through Yellowstone in a day. How does one cover 3,468 square miles and 237 miles of main highway in a day? I figured out that the best way to do this is to balance breadth and depth. I drove most of the main highways so that my friends could see dozens of major features. Yet I made four or five key stops—Old Faithful, Mammoth Hot Springs, the Fountain Paint Pots, and the Grand Canyon of the Yellowstone—so that my friends could explore these areas a bit more fully.

A similar approach works with preaching the Gospels. For example, with the "lost" stories in Luke 15, the three parables clearly go together, so preaching them together will help listeners keep the big picture in mind. Yet the parable of the lost, or prodigal, son is so compelling that it seems to deserve a sermon of its own. In fact, the parable could be the grist for more than one sermon. Timothy Keller's book *The Prodigal God* reflects a way to break it down into seven sermons.[13] So what is a preacher to do—three parables in one sermon, one parable in one sermon, or one parable in seven sermons? The answer is all of the above. Vary your approach over time and even within a series on a particular Gospel.

Personally I prefer to preach all three "lost" stories together. I want people to get a good sense of the flow of Luke's argument. If, however, I turn to Luke 15 to address the meaning of salvation or the way that we are to view our unchurched neighbors, then I will tend to focus solely on the third parable.

The last three kingdom parables in Matthew 13:44–52 present a similar challenge. I have preached the three together in a sermon titled "Life in God's Kingdom: Priceless." But I have also preached basically the same sermon by concentrating on Matthew 13:44–45, on the two brief parables of the hidden treasure and the pearl. By working with such a small unit of two verses, I was able to develop the images at greater length.

Even in a series where I tend to take larger chunks of the story, I will work the balance between breadth and depth by occasionally taking a shorter-than-usual text. Sometimes a pericope, or unit of text, happens to be unusually short. This is certainly the case with Mark 12:41–44, the story of the widow's offering. While this story might be grouped with the preceding stories about Jesus' debates with the teachers of the law, so that Mark 12:28–44 becomes a preaching unit,[14] it is most natural to devote a single sermon to this brief but powerful text.

Of course, it makes sense at other times to combine texts that are often preached separately. For example, when preaching through Luke, it seems natural to preach a sermon on the parable of the Good Samaritan (Luke 10:25–37) and then a sermon on Jesus' words to Martha when he visited her and her sister, Mary (Luke 10:38–42). However, there may be a good reason to preach these two pericopes together. Jesus' parable of the Good Samaritan is basically his way of answering, "Who is my neighbor?" This question came from an expert in the law who wanted to justify himself when Jesus challenged him to love God and love his neighbor (Luke 10:27). Jesus' challenge to Martha and his commendation of Mary has to do with the command to "love the Lord your God with all your heart and with all your soul and with all your strength and with all your mind" (Luke 10:27). So preaching the two pericopes together will help listeners see the connection between loving God and neighbor. The main movements in such a sermon might look like this:

> Variety is the key. Survey the overall terrain, but stop once in a while to drill deeper.

5. Determine what you leave on your desk and why.

Preaching through entire Gospels will require you to preach longer texts; preaching longer texts will require you to leave some material on your desk or hard drive. I am writing this section a few hours after preaching Luke 3:1–20. This is a magnificent text on repentance. But to preach it as one unit, I had to leave a lot of material on my desk. Here are some issues that I mentioned only briefly, in one or two sentences, without any development:

- The origin of John's baptism—proselyte baptism, Qumran, or something new (v. 3)
- Isaiah's "new exodus" in Isaiah 40:3–5 as quoted by Luke (vv. 4–6)
- What exactly a tunic is (v. 11)
- The system of tax collection in first-century Palestine (v. 12)
- What kind of soldiers Jesus was addressing since his crowd was Jewish (v. 14)
- Whether Jesus' baptism with the Holy Spirit and fire is one or two baptisms (v. 16)
- Background information on winnowing wheat (v. 17)

- Background information on the sins of Herod the tetrarch (vv. 19–20)

But what kind of grid must a preacher use to decide what to leave on the table? In his classic textbook *Biblical Preaching,* Haddon Robinson counsels preachers who have identified the main idea communicated by a biblical text to ask three developmental questions. These questions should be applied both to the text and to our listeners. We are trying to discover which question(s) the biblical writer addressed and which question(s) our listeners will have when they read the passage.

1. The explanation question: what does it mean?
2. The validation or "proof" question: is it true?
3. The application question: what difference does it make?[15]

To be honest, the first time I read Robinson's discussion about these questions, I dismissed it as a mechanical, formulaic piece of busy work. Years later I realized how brilliant these questions really are. They are all about how thought forms. They are about how writers and speakers develop ideas. Furthermore, the questions are logically sequential. You cannot accept what you do not understand. You cannot apply what you don't accept.

I apply the questions to the biblical text to understand how the writer developed his thought, but applying them to my listeners helps me determine which material to include and which material to leave out of my sermon. I simply ask: as I preach this text, what must I explain, what must I validate, and what must I apply? I am trying to anticipate where my listeners will say, "I don't understand that," or, "I'm not sure I buy into that idea," or, "I am not sure what difference that makes in my life."

Since repentance is a major theme in Luke 3:1–20, I sensed that my listeners needed the concept explained. After all, repentance is not part of our day-to-day vocabulary. So I took some time to develop it. At the same time, I did not see the need to go into a lengthy explanation of tax collection in first-century Palestine. Instead of overexplaining, I simply said: "When tax collectors in Jesus' day collected tax for the government, they were allowed to collect extra for themselves. This was their salary. But these collectors often charged ridiculous amounts and found ways to manipulate and even threaten citizens." Then I moved on to the next issue in the text. I could have given a lot of fascinating information about the leasing of tax districts and the details as to how tax collectors cheated those in their districts, but it was not necessary for understanding the text.

As I thought about where my listeners might need validation, I thought about John calling the crowds a brood of vipers (Luke 3:7). This seems a bit over the top. So I took a minute to talk about how the crowds would have consisted of religious people who were relying on their religious heritage but taking advantage of other people. I also thought about how some listeners would have a hard time buying into the idea of harsh treatment for those who did not produce good fruit (Luke 3:9). But I decided that this was not the place to validate the idea of God's judgment of those who do evil.

Interestingly, I have heard Haddon Robinson refer to this second question, the one pertaining to validation, as the "C. S. Lewis question." Lewis was masterful at anticipating and answering objections about the Christian faith. Today Timothy Keller is a good example of a preacher who works this question well. His book *The Reason for God* not only provides good content but also models how preachers can approach the most common objections to the Christian faith in their preaching.

Finally, as I thought about where my listeners might need help with application, I realized they needed modern examples of "fruit in keeping with repentance" (Luke 3:8). The challenges John subsequently offers to the three different groups—the crowd, the tax collectors, and the soldiers—have in common a concern for treating others generously and fairly without taking advantage of them. So I challenged my listeners to turn from a self-centered use of their time and wealth to participation in some specific opportunities we provide to help those in need in our community. I challenged my listeners to stop verbal abuse such as gossip or criticism and to replace it with gracious speech. I challenged my listeners not to take advantage of workers—even volunteers in a ministry situation!—but to give them reasonable pay and a reasonable pace, praying for them and encouraging them as needed.

The bottom line is to be intentional about what you include in your message and what you leave on the cutting-room floor for another occasion. Make sure you are answering the questions your listeners will ask or should ask—not just the ones you find fascinating.

6. Reading the Scripture well is a key part of preaching and helps listeners digest longer texts.

Scripture reading is the missing jewel in much contemporary evangelical preaching. Think about the sermon you heard or preached last weekend. How well was the Scripture read? If you were the one preaching, how much time did you spend preparing yourself or someone else to read the text? Oddly enough, we go to great lengths to prepare sermons, but we spend little time preparing to read the text. This is not surprising, I suppose, given the fact that just about anyone, let alone pastors, can read off the cuff. Yet there is a place for the expository *reading* of Scripture. It can enrich worshipers whether or not it is connected to a sermon, but it especially serves us well when we preach the longer texts in the Gospels.

I first heard the expression "expository reading of Scripture" at a seminar by Reg Grant, a professor of pastoral ministries at Dallas Theological Seminary. He challenged pastors to stop reading words into the page of Scripture. Instead, he told us to look people in the eye and to read the biblical text—a text that we had diligently studied and read out loud at least a dozen times. Grant added: "When you read well, retention is higher. When you read well, people will say, 'I've never *seen* it that way before.' As an old Arab proverb says, 'Good reading turns the ear into an eye.'"[16]

A few years later, I had the opportunity to read Scripture for Max McLean and receive a critique. McLean is an actor who has received acclaim for his off-Broadway, solo theatrical performances, including his performance of the Gospel of Mark. Not long ago he performed it at Chicago's Mercury Theater. My opportunity came in a doctoral seminar on preaching. Our professor Haddon Robinson invited McLean to spend a day with us and critique our reading. I would like to say that I impressed McLean with my stellar reading of the biblical text assigned to me. But he gently scolded me and the others in our seminar for reading the text in a way that reflected little preparation.

Like Reg Grant, McLean advocates eye contact. He remarked, "The eyes are the window to your soul. So before reading a text publicly, read it through at least eight times so that you know it very well. If you do not know it well, you will not be able to maintain eye contact."[17]

But eye contact is only one payoff for careful preparation on the part of the Scripture reader. Passionate delivery of your reading is another benefit. Listeners need to hear the fear in a word like *afraid*. They also need to hear the different voices in the text. McLean observed: "A simple pause after a 'he said' or 'Jesus said' will help listeners distinguish between the narrator's voice and the character's voice." Without careful preparation, preachers or others who read Scripture can do "an extraordinary amount of subtle damage, sending a subconscious message that Scripture reading is not important."

Every portion of Scripture, whether long or short, deserves to be well read. Yet this is even more pressing when a preacher has a longer text from the Gospels. Reading a gospel selection well can help listeners digest the words and concepts that a preacher may not take time to explain due to the length of the selected text.

Whenever I discuss Scripture reading with pastors, three questions get raised. The first is, how much of a long text should I read? Do I read it all, or can I read only key parts of it? My preference is to read the entire passage word for word. But when a preacher has reason to keep a long text together, such as John 6:1–71, or combine a couple of related stories, such as in Mark 5:1–43, it may be necessary to summarize parts and read only the dialogue or the key statements made by the narrator. So summarize well and read well.

A second question is, when should I read the text? Should I read it all at the beginning of my sermon, or should I read the various parts of the text as the sermon progresses? I like to vary

my approach. Sometimes I read an entire passage or have someone else read it at the beginning of my sermon—either before or
after the sermon's introduction. This allows people to hear the
whole account as it was written. This cultivates a reverence for
the Scripture and challenges people to listen. I do not buy the
idea that it gives away the ending; most people know the ending
already. There is something satisfying and stirring about hearing
the ending to a story we have heard several times before.

There are times when I want to read the text in sections as
the sermon progresses. With this approach, I will often weave
my explanatory comments into the reading. The downside is
that listeners do not hear the whole account all at once. Still,
carefully crafted, carefully timed comments may reveal rather
than obscure the flow of a story or a teaching of Jesus. On occasion, I will even read an account at the end of a sermon. The
benefit is that it keeps the passage intact, yet it allows listeners
to hear the account after it has been explained to them and after
they have been exhorted by it.

A third question is, who should read the Scripture? Should
preachers reserve this for themselves or involve others? Once
again, both approaches are legitimate. It is a matter of preference. By reading it ourselves, we can demonstrate how much we
treasure the Scripture through a passionate, accurate rendition.
Alternatively, by assigning the reading of Scripture to someone
else, preachers can make use of the gifts of others, thereby dem-
onstrating the unity of believers. If you listen to a sermon by
Timothy Keller delivered at Redeemer Presbyterian Church in
New York City, you will most likely be moved by the readings of
Scripture executed by men and women who are part of the congregation. Whether or not your congregation has such a high
caliber of readers—some of whom are trained in theater—you

can bring the best out of the readers you select by listening to them read and then coaching them before your worship services. Occasionally you can even combine approaches and invite readers to read with you. I did this recently when I preached on Luke 1:39–56, covering Elizabeth's blessing of Mary and Mary's song. I served as the narrator, reading verses 39–42a, 46a, and 56. Then I invited a middle-aged woman to read Elizabeth's blessing in verses 42b–45. Finally I asked a fourteen-year-old who possessed poise and good reading skills to handle Mary's Magnificat in verses 46b–55. Hearing the words of Mary read by a young lady who was roughly Mary's age when she gave birth to Jesus was stunning. The entire reading of the text was so moving that I was tempted to sit down when we had finished! But I am confident that my sermon was better simply because listeners had *seen* the text through our reading of it.

Preaching the Gospels will require some longer-than-usual texts and longer-than-usual sermon series. But working with the above six theses can help you plan series and preach sermons that give people a fine grasp of the overall good news of Jesus—who he is, what he did, and what he said.

2

ARE JESUS AND PAUL ON THE SAME PAGE?

*How to interpret the Gospels in relation
to the rest of the New Testament*

One of the first challenges preachers face when preparing to preach the Gospels is understanding how the Gospels relate to the rest of the New Testament—specifically Acts and the Epistles. A cursory reading of the New Testament reveals some marked differences between Jesus, or the Evangelists who record his works and words, and Paul—not to mention the authors of the remaining Epistles. Jesus talks a lot about repentance; Paul does not. Jesus talks a lot about the kingdom of God, while Paul says little about it. Paul develops the idea of "the flesh" as under the control of evil impulses and the idea of sinners being dead in their sin, yet this "radical language" does not appear in the Gospels.[1]

The problem cannot be explained by a mere development in the understanding of Jesus' life and teaching. While the Gospels give accounts of events that took place *before* Jesus' ascension, the Evangelists who composed them did so *after* Jesus' ascension. In fact, the Gospels were written *after* most of the New Testament Epistles were penned by the apostle Paul and others.[2] The Gospels "all are written from a post-Easter standpoint and know that the Christian church continues to exist, committed to the mission entrusted to it by Jesus."[3]

In a 2010 *Christianity Today* cover story, "Jesus vs. Paul," Scot McKnight claims: "It is not exaggerating to say that evangelicalism is facing a crisis about the relationship of Jesus to Paul, and that many today are choosing sides."[4] The "first language" of one side is Jesus and the kingdom, while the other side speaks the language of Paul and justification. "Those addicted to kingdom language struggle to make Paul fit, while those addicted to Paul's theological terms struggle to make Jesus fit."[5]

So are Jesus and Paul at odds? Is there irreconcilable diversity among the Gospels and the Epistles—both the Pauline Epistles and the General Epistles? Does Jesus' theology contradict Paul's theology? Before preaching any of the four Gospels, a preacher must be able to answer these questions. The answer, I suggest, resembles the answer to the question I used to hear as a resident of Montana: is the state of Montana a place of irreconcilable diversity and contradiction?

The reason for this question is not a mystery. As one who traveled almost every highway in Montana and visited almost every one of its towns during a quarter of a century of ministry there, I found its diversity remarkable. The eastern half of the state consists of grassland, much of it desolate prairie. Sage brush dots the landscape, with cottonwood trees lining the rivers. But in western Montana, rugged mountain ranges dominate the landscape with snow-capped peaks towering over fertile valleys. Some have wondered if West Dakota would be a more apt name for eastern Montana! Then there is the clash between life in the cities and in the rural communities. Bozeman, for example, is home to Montana State University, software companies, and at least one laser technology company. Folks living in little towns like Wilsall and Cardwell—both within an hour's drive of Bozeman—are predominantly ranchers, loggers, and miners. Yes, there is diversity.

Yet I have observed a unique unity that binds the state together. The population density is small throughout the state. The climate is cold, dry, and windy. The view of the big sky is just as striking in the western valleys as it is in the eastern plains. Politically the state forms one huge congressional district. Whether you buy blue jeans, pizza, or a leather sofa in Miles City (in the east) or in Missoula (in the west), there is no sales tax. This list could go on and on. As one of my friends, a lifetime Montanan, told me, "We all know our place. Some of us are city Montanans, some of us are country Montanans. But we are all Montanans." Esteemed New Testament scholar I. Howard Marshall wants to stress the same point about the New Testament. The subtitle of his magnificent *New Testament Theology* puts it well: *Many Witnesses, One Gospel.*

This chapter will explore how to understand the Gospels in relation to the rest of the New Testament—both the book of Acts and the New Testament Epistles penned by Paul and others. I will argue for an overarching consistency and unity in the message of the Evangelists and Epistle writers. The diversity between the Gospels and the rest of the New Testament, I propose, does not reflect fundamental differences in theology but rather differences in literary genre, purpose, audience, and authorial personality.

What Binds the New Testament Corpus Together

So what leads us to believe there is a harmonious relationship between the Gospels and the rest of the New Testament, rather than irreconcilable diversity? Interestingly, both I. Howard Marshall and Scot McKnight, the two New Testament scholars already cited who have wrestled deeply with this issue, point to the *same* Scripture text to identify what binds the New Testament corpus together. This Scripture text is 1 Corinthians 15:1–11:

> Now, brothers and sisters, I want to remind you of the gospel I preached to you, which you received and on which you have taken your stand. By this gospel you are saved, if you hold firmly to the word I preached to you. Otherwise, you have believed in vain.

> For what I received I passed on to you as of first importance: that Christ died for our sins according to the Scriptures, that he was buried, that he was raised on the third day according to the Scriptures, and that he appeared to Cephas, and then to the Twelve. After that, he appeared to more than five hundred of the brothers and sisters at the same time, most of whom are still living, though some have fallen asleep. Then he appeared to James, then to all the apostles, and last of all he appeared to me also, as to one abnormally born.

> For I am the least of the apostles and do not even deserve to be called an apostle, because I persecuted the church of God. But by the grace of God I am what I am, and his grace to me was not without effect. No, I worked harder than all of them, yet not I, but the grace of God that was with me. Whether, then, it is I or they, this is what we preach, and this is what you believed.

What, then, provides an underlying unity for the New Testament Gospels, book of Acts, and the Letters? The answer is "the gospel." According to Marshall, this text "affirms that he [Paul] and the first followers of Jesus preached one and the same gospel."[6] Likewise, McKnight comments: "Behind or underneath both kingdom and justification is the gospel, and the gospel is *the saving story of Jesus that completes Israel's story.*"[7] Paul's vision of justification by faith dominates his preaching, while Jesus used the term *justified* as Paul did only once.[8] Yet Paul preached the same gospel as Jesus because Paul preached the saving story of Jesus centered in Jesus' death and resurrection. Jesus' vision of the kingdom dominated his preaching so much so that the Synoptic Gospels present him as preaching "the gospel of the kingdom" (see Matt. 4:23; 9:35; Mark 1:15; Luke 4:43; 16:16). Yet Jesus preached the same gospel as Paul because Jesus preached himself. In fact, the end of the book of Acts tells us that when Paul arrived in Rome to make his appeal to Caesar, he spent his time explaining and preaching the kingdom of God (28:23, 31).

It is important to note the continuity of the gospel message as it goes from Jesus to Paul. Marshall explains: "The gospel is a given, handed down to Paul by other Christians, and there is no evidence of any dispute with the leaders in Jerusalem over its essential contents."[9] This is an important point given the account in Acts 15 of a dispute brought to the church at Jerusalem over whether Gentile believers needed to be circumcised. Had there been a dispute over the basic gospel message, we would expect the Jerusalem Council to have dealt with it and Luke to have recorded it. Marshall then summarizes how the "content of the gospel" is "centered on the death and resurrection of Jesus, understood as the means through which people can be delivered from their sins and God's judgment upon them. The death of Jesus . . . is an act of deliverance or redemption that sets sinners free from their sin." Marshall concludes: "This understanding can be traced back to the teaching of Jesus as recorded in the synoptic Gospels, where his death is understood as a ransom for many and as having a sacrificial character (Mk 10:45; 14:24)."[10]

Two other observations may be helpful. First, as McKnight points out, "there's not a word here [in 1 Corinthians 15:1–8] about either kingdom or justification!"[11] While these are both key ways of framing and explicating the gospel, neither by itself tells the entire story. So there is no need to fret over an alleged contradiction as if the message of kingdom and the message of justification are different messages. Both explicate the same gospel. Second, according to Marshall, "although some modern scholars tend to write as if the various New Testament authors lived on separate islands with no contact with other known figures, . . . Galatians 1–2 places it beyond any doubt that James, John, Paul, and Peter knew each other and talked together, and in the immortal phrase of C. H. Dodd, 'we may presume they did not spend all the time talking about the weather.'"[12]

What Accounts for the Differences between the Gospels and the Epistles

Once we establish the gospel, or good news of God's saving activity in Christ, as the underlying unity that binds the Gospels and Epistles together, it is not difficult to account for the differences between them. Three observations are helpful here.

First, the New Testament is composed of "occasional" documents. What Gordon Fee says about the New Testament Epistles certainly applies to the Gospels as well. Each New Testament book, whether a gospel or an epistle, "is an *ad hoc* document, that is, a piece of correspondence occasioned by a set of specific historical circumstances, either from the recipient's or author's side—or both."[13]

Marshall shows how this accounts for the differences between Paul's Epistles and the Gospel of John. "The theology of Paul is constituted in part by the debate with the Judaizers and with proponents of a way of thinking that was more indebted to Hellenistic ways of thinking that emphasized wisdom, knowledge and human status." As we might expect, "these matters are much less to the fore in the Gospel of John, where the dispute is much more with the synagogue and its rejection of Jesus as the Messiah and where the more specific issues of life within the church are not a primary concern."[14]

Furthermore, we should expect different emphases on the part of the gospel writers and the writers of the Epistles for no other reason than the differences we find within Paul's own epistles! Marshall observes that there is less material on the pervasiveness of sin in Paul's other letters than in Romans.[15] Yet we do not fret over this, as if we assumed that Paul must delve into all aspects of his theology at the same level of detail in every piece of his correspondence. Nor must we fret over this when Jesus says much about repentance and Paul says little about it. Both make the same points with different images.

Second, the literary genre itself accounts for some of the differences. Matthew, Mark, Luke, and John are telling stories rather than writing letters.[16] They communicate their message by narrating Jesus' evangelistic mission rather than by offering specific instructions as Paul does in his letters for the upbuilding of congregations.

Third, we should expect the authors' personalities and gifts to lead to differences in content. Nowhere is this more clear than in the differences between Luke and Paul. Luke is a bridge between Jesus and Paul, having written extensive accounts about both—Jesus in Luke's Gospel and Paul in Luke's sequel called the

Acts of the Apostles. Noting the differences between the Paul of Acts (written by Luke) and the Paul of the letters (written by Paul), Marshall observes that "Luke did not have the depth of theological insight possessed by Paul. There is no point at which he contradicts Paul, but equally he does not share Paul's profundity."[17] Marshall provides a helpful analogy here. He argues that Paul's theology is the same as Luke's theology but is stated at a different level, "just as a high Anglican liturgical service with its elaborate ritual and use of centuries of Christian language and music may have the same shape and content as a simple non-liturgical service that expresses an identical faith and experience in a different mode."[18]

When Jesus Seems to Preach Works-Righteousness

Still, despite all the talk of diversity within a fundamental unity, preachers of the Gospels—let alone readers!—are troubled by texts in which Jesus seems to preach works-righteousness rather than faith as the means of receiving God's salvation. A brief survey of two especially problematic teachings can help us see that Jesus' message, though articulated at times a bit differently than Paul's, is still an offer of salvation by grace through faith and not as a result of works. To keep the survey brief, I will limit the discussion to these teachings as they are recorded in Matthew's Gospel. What we discover there will help us read the parallel accounts in Luke's Gospel as well as various texts in the other Gospels that seem to hint at works-righteousness.

The first challenging text brings Jesus' Sermon on the Mount in Matthew 5–7 to a stirring conclusion. According to Matthew 7:21, Jesus announces:

> Not everyone who says to me, "Lord, Lord," will enter the kingdom of heaven, but only the one who does the will of my Father who is in heaven. Many will say to me on that day, "Lord, Lord did we not prophesy in your name and in your name drive out demons and in your name perform many miracles?" Then I will tell them plainly, "I never knew you. Away from me, you evildoers!"

Jesus concludes his sermon with a parable of the wise and foolish builders, likening those who hear and practice his words to a wise man who builds his house on the rock and thus survives the storm (Matt. 7:24–27). Has Jesus claimed that good works, or obedience, leads to salvation?

D. A. Carson wisely points readers to the context of the entire Gospel to help us understand that entrance into the kingdom turns on obedience—not one "which earns merit points, but which bows to Jesus' lordship in everything and without reservation."[19] He writes:

> We ought not to forget that Matthew's record of the Sermon on the Mount must be taken in the context of his entire Gospel. It is not for nothing that his Gospel begins with a prophecy concerning Jesus that stresses his function *as a Savior*. . . (Matt. 1:21). Within this context, the Sermon on the Mount does not press men and women to despair, still less to self-salvation. Rather, it presses men and women to Jesus.[20]

The immediate context also helps preachers navigate Jesus' strong words. David Turner observes that Matthew 7:13–27 "presents an ethical dualism that vividly and repeatedly contrasts discipleship and antinomianism." Jesus uses the imagery of two gates/ways (7:13–14), two trees/fruits (7:15–23), and two builders/foundations (7:24–27) to make this contrast—a contrast that has its roots in the Hebrew Bible and is found in Second Temple Jewish literature.[21] What Jesus says in the middle section (7:15–23) "clearly distinguishes between two kinds of fruit and two kinds of trees. This rejects any sort of 'cheap grace,' that teaches that the many who luxuriate on the broad path will somehow after all end up in the kingdom with those who make the rigorous trek of discipleship."[22] Jesus, then, is warning a group steeped in religious teaching and ritual that obedience is the *proof* of their commitment to him, not the *cause* of it.

The approach taken here will help preachers make sense of similar statements made by Jesus in Matthew 25:31–46—the so-called "parable of the sheep and the goats." As D. A. Carson notes, "the surprise of the righteous [at the reason for their admission to the kingdom] makes it impossible to think that works of righteousness win salvation."[23]

The story of the wealthy young man in Matthew 19:16–30 presents another challenge. When this man approaches Jesus and asks what "good thing" he must do to get eternal life, Jesus ends up replying: "if you want to enter life, keep the commandments" (vv. 16–17). The discussion turns to which commands, and Jesus specifies six of the "ten words" given by God to Moses (vv. 18–19). The young man claims to have kept these and asks what he still lacks (v. 20). Jesus replies with another "work." He tells the young man to sell his possessions, give to the poor, and then come follow Jesus (v. 21). This is hardly the message Jesus gives to Martha after the death of her brother, when Jesus says: "The one who believes in me will live, even though they die; and whoever lives by believing in me will never die" (John 11:25–26). So how are we to understand this?

Grant Osborne insists that "Jesus is not teaching a works righteousness within which we find eternal life by keeping the commandments."[24] Instead, Jesus "is drawing the rich young man into reflection on the reality of his life of piety, probably to get him to realize his sin." Jesus, then, is tailoring his "gospel presentation" to account for this man's divided heart. His wealth was competing with his allegiance to God. There is no suggestion that this man will be able to keep these commands. In fact, Jesus assumes otherwise. As D. A. Carson observes, "What the man needs is the triumph of grace, for as the next verses show, entering the kingdom of heaven is impossible for him [Matt. 19:26]. God, with whom all things are possible, must work. The parable in 20:1–16 directly speaks to this issue."[25]

A couple of further observations regarding faith and works are worth making. First, the Gospel of John records Jesus speaking often of faith as the means through which people receive the gift of eternal life (5:24; 6:35; 7:38; 11:25; 12:46). John himself emphasizes faith for entering God's family and possessing eternal life (1:12; 3:16, 36).

Second, the tension between faith and obedience also appears in Paul. For example, in the prescript to Paul's Epistle to the Romans (1:5), he writes: "Through him [Jesus Christ our Lord] we received grace and apostleship to call all the Gentiles to the obedience that comes from faith for his name's sake." Scholars have long debated the grammatical relationship between the terms *obedience* and *faith*. Grammatically, faith can be the source of obedience, or faith can be the definition of obedience.[26] Douglas Moo suggests understanding the words to be mutually interpreting:

Obedience always involves faith, and faith always involves obedience. They should not be equated, compartmentalized, or made into separate stages of Christian experience. Paul called men and women to a faith that was always inseparable from obedience—for the Savior in whom we believe is nothing less than our Lord—and to an obedience that could never be divorced from faith—for we can obey Jesus as Lord only when we have given ourselves to him in faith.[27]

Paul simultaneously says that our salvation is "not by works" and that "we arc God's handiwork, created in Christ Jesus to do good works" (Eph. 2:9–10). Jesus preserves this balance, too.

The New Perspective on Paul, Jesus, and Judaism

Preachers who wrestle with how to preach Gospel texts that suggest a kind of works-righteousness must back up a step and address another question. Is works-righteousness really even a problem that Jesus must address? Some New Testament scholars in the past three decades have questioned whether works-righteousness was a real problem in first-century Judaism. These scholars have presented a "new perspective" on what Paul opposes when he talks about justification by faith. The "old perspective" that grew out of the Reformation saw the problem with "works of the law" as the problem of attempting to merit God's favor by doing good works. The "new perspective," championed by the likes of James D. G. Dunn and N. T. Wright, argues that Paul did not oppose this kind of legalism because it was not a major problem in Second Temple Judaism. Rather, the problem Paul addressed was the insistence on maintaining Jewish identity of the Jewish nation through "boundary markers" such as Sabbath observance, circumcision, and eating kosher.

But what does this have to do with the Gospels? If the "new perspective" is an issue in Paul's Letters, it is as well in the

Gospels. As Simon Gathercole notes, the idea that Paul was concerned about an obsession with markers of one's Jewish heritage rather than with works-righteousness "is actually more a new perspective on Judaism than on Paul."[28] This takes us right back to Jesus. If the new perspective on Judaism is correct, then this changes our understanding of the gospel as taught by Jesus as well as the gospel as taught by Paul. We have already established from 1 Corinthians 15:1–11 that Jesus and Paul are proclaiming the same gospel.

So what are we to make of the new perspective? D. A. Carson and Douglas Moo claim that "the general tendency of the new perspective as a whole to redirect our attention to the Jewish matrix of Paul's thought and teaching is a welcome one."[29] Admittedly, the description of Judaism in Paul's (and Jesus') day by the Reformers Calvin and Luther was colored by their anxiety about Roman Catholic works-righteousness in the 1500s.[30] However, even if Calvin and Luther somewhat caricaturized Second Temple Judaism's struggle with works-righteousness, they were not entirely wrong about it either! A careful reading of writings from Second Temple Judaism shows that the problem of works-righteousness *did* exist.[31] Here is a tiny sample of text during and shortly after the Second Temple period that reflects the presence of this belief.

> The one who does what is right saves up life for himself
>   with the Lord,
> and the one who does what is wrong causes his own life to
>   be destroyed;
> for the Lord's righteous judgments are according to the
>   individual and the household.[32]
>
> (*Pss. Sol.* 9:5, ca. 50 B.C.)

Miracles, however, will appear at their own time to those who are saved because of their works and for whom the Law is now a hope, and intelligence, expectation, and wisdom a trust.[33] (*2 Bar.* 51:7, ca. A.D. 100)

For those . . . who live in accordance with our laws the prize is not silver or gold, no crown of wild olive or of parsley with any such public mark of distinction. No; each individual, relying on the witness of his own conscience and the law-giver's prophecy, confirmed by the sure testimony of God, is firmly persuaded that to those who observe the laws and, if they must needs die for them, willingly meet death, God has granted a renewed existence and in the revolution of the ages the gift of a better life.[34] (Josephus, *Against Apion* 2.217–218, A.D. ca. 97–100)

From the didactic stories in the Apocrypha (Judith, Tobit) to the apocalypses of the Pseudepigrapha (particularly *2 Enoch*), and from *The Rule of Community* in Qumran to the apologetic writings of Josephus, works-righteousness appears in various forms.[35] While Jesus emphasizes good works as a *result* and *proof* of salvation, he never attributes the *cause* of salvation as anything other than grace. For Jesus and the gospel writers who recorded his deeds and words, salvation comes through faith.

Implications for Preaching the Gospels

When preaching texts from the Gospels that seem to contradict what the Pauline or General Epistles teach, preachers can account for the differences and reconcile the alleged contradictions in the following ways.

1. Remember that the Gospels, like the Epistles, are "occasional" documents that were written to address particular issues or concerns in the life of the church. Is Jesus going after complacency or wealth or pride? If so, what he says may be different from what Paul says to the Judaizers in his letter to the Galatians.

2. Remember that the Gospels communicate theology by telling the story of Jesus' evangelistic mission rather than by offering the kind of specific instructions found in the Epistles for the edification of local churches.

3. Expect to find personality differences between the gospel writers and the writers of thc Epistles. These differences include stylistic traits, theological depth, particular concerns, and modes of expression. Some writers tend toward more measured reasoning, others toward more bombastic rhetoric.

4. Look to the context for clues as to why Jesus uses hyperbole or parable or language that seems to contradict the teaching of the Epistles. For an alert reader, Jesus' words to the wealthy young man in Matthew 19:16–30 reflect a strategy to zero in on the obstacle to faith—the young man's preoccupation with his wealth—rather than a works-righteousness kind of teaching.

5. Look to the context for an emphasis on grace. Following the report of Jesus' encounter with the rich young man (Matt. 19:16–30) is a parable that speaks to God's grace (20:1–16).

6. Remember that the gospel text you are preparing to preach is connected to the gospel story as summarized by Paul in 1 Corinthians 15:1–11.

My experience growing up was similar to that of Scot McKnight.[36] The churches in which I grew up focused on the Epistles. I heard only an occasional message on the Gospels, predictably at Christmas or Easter. I pray that God will raise up a generation of preachers who proclaim the gospel from both the Gospels and the Epistles. I pray that a new generation of preachers will show the unity of the New Testament without flattening out the differences between Paul and Jesus and show the New Testament's diversity without driving a wedge between the fundamental message proclaimed by both Paul and Jesus.

As I wrap up this chapter, I think of David, a steel broker in his late thirties who found his way to a congregation I pastored more than a decade ago. David was bright, respectful, and yet skeptical of the gospel. We frequently discussed the claims of Christ over coffee. He had a philosophical bent, so I suggested that he read *Mere Christianity* by C. S. Lewis. Still, he would not budge from his skepticism. A couple of years into our discussion, David showed up on a Sunday when I preached Mark 10:17–31—yes, the story of the rich man who was instructed by Jesus to sell all of his possessions and give to the poor. David had heard me preach dozens of sermons prior to this day. But this is the sermon that God used to bring David to faith. Instead of creating confusion between what David had read and heard from the Epistles, this text crystallized everything David had heard before about salvation by grace through faith and not works. It exposed the last obstacle to his unbelief—material wealth. After the worship service, David sought out one of our leaders who had also developed a relationship with Jesus. The two talked for half an hour, and David moved from unbelief to belief.

There is no contradiction between the message of the Gospel and the Epistles. Personality differences on the part of the writers? Yes. Varied theological emphases and pastoral concerns being addressed? Yes. Different literary forms and thus different strategies? Yes. A different message? No. What Marshall says about Paul and John applies more broadly to the Epistles and the Gospels: "We have two different artists or schools of artists who see the same subject in different ways, but it is the same subject, and we need both sets of pictures to bring out the richness of the common theme."[37]

3

BACKGROUND CHECK

*Rightly handling the Jewish and Greco-
Roman context of the Gospels*

Time magazine in 2008 listed the rereading of the Gospels through Jewish eyes as one of the "10 ideas that are changing the world." According to an article titled "Re-Judaizing Jesus," Christian pastors and scholars insist that to understand Jesus you have to understand first-century Judaism.[1] As Vanderbilt University New Testament scholar Amy-Jill Levine claims, "If you get the [Jewish] context wrong, you will certainly get Jesus wrong."[2] But how to understand first-century Judaism remains a point of contention.

For example, Rob Bell, the former megachurch pastor whose books and *Nooma* videos have engaged thousands of twenty- and thirty-somethings, raises this question in his popular book *Velvet Elvis*: "Did Jesus go to school and learn like the other Jewish kids his age?"[3] Bell suggests that Jesus received a rigorous education in the Scriptures early in his childhood—a point no Christian scholar would dispute. Then he goes into detail, describing how students with natural abilities in the Scriptures would distance themselves from the others and go to the next level of education called *Bet Talmud* (House of Learning).[4] *Bet*

Talmud began around age ten and lasted until about age four-teen. This certainly helps us make sense of the occasion when Jesus' parents found him sitting in the temple courts among the teachers, listening to them and asking them questions (Luke 2:41–50). Jesus was twelve at the time.

Bell then notes that "around the age of fourteen, at the end of *Bet Talmud*, only the best of the best were still studying."[5] Most were learning the family business or starting their own families. The brightest went on to a level of education known as *Bet Midrash* (House of Study). This involved leaving one's parents and following a rabbi everywhere. Rabbis were selective about whom they admitted into such a rigorous training process. Bell surmises that when Jesus called Peter, Andrew, James, and John, they were fishermen and not good enough to be disciples of a rabbi. The upshot is that "Jesus took some boys who didn't make the cut and changed the course of human history."[6] Now this will preach!

But hold on for a moment. New Testament scholar Ben Witherington sounds a note of caution. He challenges Bell's understanding of early Judaism in the time of Jesus:

> In the first place, Jesus was no rabbi. So far as we can tell, there is no archaeological evidence at all for bet Talmud or bet Midrash in Jesus' day in Galilee. There were some schools in Jerusalem, but they were far from Galilee. . . . In fact, you will notice that Jesus has no encounters with "rabbis." Scribes yes, Pharisees yes, Sadducees yes, priests yes, synagogue Presidents like Jairus yes—but no rabbis. This is because there were no ordained rabbis hanging around synagogues in Jesus' day. It is a huge mistake to read the Talmuds and the Mishnah as if they were describing the world that

Jesus lived in, when in fact they mostly described Judaism after the two Jewish wars when Judaism had been whittled down mostly to Pharisaism and had become a much more Torah-centric religion. Jesus was not a rabbi, nor did he have close encounters of the first kind with ordained rabbis. There were none in his day.[7]

So where has Rob Bell gone wrong? Witherington minces no words:

> At times Rob [Bell] seems too uncritical in his reading of sources like the truly dated works of Alfred Edersheim, and apparently he spends too much time listening to folks like Ray Vanderlaan [sic], a local teacher in the Grand Rapids area who doesn't really much understand the differences between medieval Jewish rabbis and the context and ethos of teachers in early Judaism of Jesus' day.[8]

The concern for getting the historical-cultural background right extends to the Greco-Roman background as well. For example, when I spent some time in Israel a few years ago, I visited the magnificent ruins of the temple of Pan at Caesarea Philippi. Jesus brought his disciples there and pressed them as to his identity. When Peter confessed Jesus as the Messiah, Jesus blessed Peter, promised the establishment of his church, and affirmed that "the gates of hades" will not prevail against it (Matt. 16:13–18). I remember my guide pointing to the arch-shaped opening at the base of a massive wall of rock adjacent to the site of the temple of Pan. Here clear water emerged from a spring. As my guide pointed, he said: "This is what Jesus meant by 'the gates of hades.' The Greeks thought that the gods lived in and emerged from this spring. Jesus uses this image from this pagan site to affirm that Satan and his forces will not overcome the church." Fascinating!

When I queried my guide about this identification, he referred me to Ray Vander Laan, the Bible teacher whose video series *That the World May Know* has enthralled small groups and Sunday school classes with the world of the Bible and how it opens up for us the meaning of the text. Rob Bell credits Ray Vander Laan as "the person who has opened me up to the first century world of Jesus more than anyone."[9] It's not surprising, then, that Bell comments as well on the significance of Caesarea Philippi as the setting for Jesus' powerful statement. He writes: "There is a cliff with a giant crack in it that the followers of Pan believed was the place where the spirits from hell would come and go from the earth. The crack was called the Gates of Hell."[10]

It is certainly significant that Jesus took his disciples to such a pagan center. It would resemble Jesus' taking present-day disciples to the strip in Las Vegas—Caesar's Palace, perhaps—and affirming that the idols of our culture will not prevail against the church. Rob Bell may well be right when he says: "As good Jewish boys, they [the disciples] never would have gone to this place before. It is twenty-six miles from Galilee, where Jesus and his disciples are from."[11] But is the "gates of hades" image to be identified strictly with the spring or the crack in the cliff?

The best and most recent commentaries on the Gospel of Matthew understand the "gates of hades" as a reference to death and dying based on the use of this expression in the Old Testament and noncanonical Jewish writings shortly before the time of Christ.[12] These commentaries are not unaware that Jesus brought his disciples to pagan territory where people worshiped the Greek god Pan.[13] Yet they insist that "gates of hades" speaks of triumph over death rather than evil spirits.[14] Ironically, Ben

Witherington is the lone, well-known evangelical commentator who comments on the relevance of the setting for understanding "gates of hades." He observes:

> At Caesarea Philippi an underground stream surfaced and can still be seen today. There were traditions that this was one of the gates to the underworld and the river Styx. Both the saying of Peter and the saying of Jesus take on special relevance and poignancy if they were given in the locale of all these shrines to other sons of the gods and next to the river thought to go into the underworld.[15]

Yet even Witherington identifies the phrase *gates of hades* as a "typical early Jewish phrase referring not to hell but to the gates of the land of the dead, the doorway into the grave so to speak."[16] So what we have at the most is a double entendre of sorts. Jesus may be simultaneously using a stock phrase from Jewish literature—including the Old Testament—and a phrase that is significant in light of the pagan place of worship he and his disciples are visiting when he talks about the gates of hades. But the use of the expression in Jewish Scripture and literature is too strong to be ignored as the key determinant of meaning.

Our concern as preachers is how we rightly understand the world in which Jesus lived and taught so we rightly understand Jesus' words and actions. Specifically, how does a preacher get accurate cultural background information? How does a preacher know when certain insights into Jewish or Greco-Roman culture are "too good to be true"?

Getting accurate information without going overboard is not as daunting as it seems. Essentially, preachers can get good information and stay within proper bounds through four practices. Each of these practices builds upon the other.

Thus preachers who are crunched for time can pursue just the first and second practices. These practices alone will provide preachers with accurate, usable information. Those who wish to go further can move into the third and fourth practices as time allows.

1. Look first for any Old Testament precedents.

Lest we overlook the obvious, preachers should begin by looking for any Old Testament precedents. Is Jesus or a gospel writer alluding to material in the Old Testament? For example, the opening sentence of Mark (1:1–2) clearly invites us to view the ministry of Jesus in the framework of prophecies by Isaiah and Malachi about a dramatic act of salvation by God.

To make such a connection, a preacher needs only to pay attention to marginal references contained in most English Bibles. The United Bible Society's edition of *The Greek New Testament* has an "Index of Quotations" that is helpful—particularly the section that follows the "New Testament Order" in which these quotations appear.

To pick up more subtle allusions, preachers will find help in the *Commentary on the New Testament Use of the Old Testament* edited by G. K. Beale and D. A. Carson. Do not be intimidated by the size of this volume; the discussions are clear and concise. Occasionally a preacher may wish to consult a more specialized work such as *Isaiah's New Exodus in Mark* by Rikki E. Watts. These works can be identified by paying attention to the citations and bibliographies in Beale and Carson's commentary. Of course, the standard commentaries on the Gospels provide this same kind of help, and this provides a good segue way into the next practice.

2. Use a handful of the most respected commentaries.

One of the best practices for getting an accurate understanding of the historical-cultural background of the Gospels is to use a handful of the most respected commentaries. Commentators are the friends of pastors. To be sure, we must do our own study and reading of the text before we grab a commentary from our bookshelf. But if we believe that God has given teachers to help equip the church (Eph. 4:11–12), why would we ignore the insights of those who have given their lives to the mastery of the biblical text?

Here, though, we run into a problem. A Jewish friend of mine who served as a pastor—though he preferred to be called rabbi—of a messianic congregation once complained to me that Jewish scholars have been ignored by the church's scholars. The implication is that mainstream New Testament scholarship over the years amounts to a "good old boys" club that has kept out Jewish scholars and their insights. The result is that the current crop of New Testament commentaries has missed certain nuances of the Gospels that come to light when viewed through Jewish culture. However, this charge is simply unfounded. If you peruse any of the best contemporary evangelical commentaries on the Gospels, you will find constant references to ancient Jewish writers (Josephus and Philo) and documents (the Apocrypha, the Dead Sea Scrolls, the Mishnah) that shed light on the world of the first century in which the events of the Gospels transpired.

In fact, Ray Vander Laan and Rob Bell are not the only folks in Grand Rapids, Michigan, who are looking to Jewish culture to provide insights into the Gospels. David Turner, professor of New Testament at Grand Rapids Theological Seminary and author of a recent 828-page commentary on the Gospel of Matthew, has a keen interest in Second Temple Judaism[17] and its role in helping exegetes understand the New Testament. Even after earning two masters' degrees and a doctorate in biblical and theological studies, he enrolled in Hebrew Union College where he earned a master's degree and a Ph.D. from the Jewish Institute of Religion. He observes that "anachronistic use of rabbinics is pervasive" in popular interpretation of the Gospels and counsels exegetes to recognize "the diverse groups that composed the Judaism of Jesus' day." He frequently gets questions about the insights of Bell and Vander Laan, and he replies: "Ask these brothers what ancient sources they are using." So, while we can hope for more scholarly research in the Gospels from Jewish believers, we need not fear that the best contemporary evangelical commentaries are missing information that will revolutionize our understanding of the Gospels.

So what commentaries should pastors consult? I have provided several recommendations in the following paragraphs for all four Gospels. Ideally pastors will consult at least two or three of them each time they study a text. When several commentators point out a particular piece of Jewish or Greco-Roman background, a pastor can be more certain about the validity of that information for understanding the text.

Matthew

For the Gospel of Matthew, David Turner's volume in the Baker Exegetical Commentary on the New Testament (hereafter BECNT) is a great place to begin. D. A. Carson's commentary on Matthew in the Expositor's Bible Commentary series (hereafter EBC) is superb as well. It was from Carson's commentary that I first learned how Matthew used the Jewish practice of gematria to shape his genealogy according to the numeric value of David's name.[18] *The Gospel of Matthew: A Socio-Rhetorical Commentary* by Craig S. Keener is especially helpful because Keener is an expert in biblical background and the volume is quite recent with a publication date of 2009.[19]

Ben Witherington's volume in the Smyth & Helwys Bible Commentary series, cited earlier, is sensitive to and sensible about background information. Other commentaries on Matthew that do an excellent job with historical-cultural background include those by Craig Blomberg (the New American Commentary series, hereafter NAC), R. T. France (the New International Commentary on the New Testament series, hereafter NICNT), Donald A. Hagner (Word Biblical Commentary series, hereafter WBC), and W. D. Davies and Dale C. Allison (International Critical Commentary series, hereafter ICC).

Mark

For the Gospel of Mark, William Lane's NICNT volume is still an outstanding classic. When I was a young pastor preaching through Mark for the first time, Lane helped me understand how the term *gospel* was not coined by Christians. Rather, "the concept was significant both in pagan and Jewish culture."[20] For example, it was frequently used in the Roman world to refer to events such as the birthday of Caesar Augustus, whose birthday was for the world "the beginning of good news." Based on this usage, Lane concludes that "the beginning of the gospel" or "good news" in Mark 1:1 refers to "an historical event which introduces a new situation for the world." And Jesus' coming is good news as it brings about a "radically new state of affairs for mankind."[21]

The more recent work by R. T. France in the New International Greek Testament Commentary series (hereafter NIGTC) is also a must-read. The two WBC volumes by Robert Guelich (Mark 1:1–8:26) and Craig Evans (8:27–16:20) contain a massive amount of information. Evans has distinguished himself as a leading expert on the Jewish background of the New Testament. Other worthwhile commentaries include *The Gospel of Mark: A Socio-Rhetorical Commentary* by Ben Witherington and the volumes by Morna Hooker (Black's New Testament Commentary series), James Edwards (Pillar), and James Brooks (NAC).

Luke

For the Gospel of Luke, Darrell Bock's massive two-volume work in the BECNT series is a gold mine of information. It builds upon the classic work by I. Howard Marshall in the NIGTC series. Both commentaries helped me correct an exegetical fallacy I committed the first time I preached the narrative of Christ's birth in Luke 2:1–20. I had read somewhere that shepherds in Jesus' day were generally not trustworthy. In fact, they had such a reputation for dishonesty that they were not allowed to testify in court. Believe me, that preached! I talked about the irony of this situation and how it underscored the point that Jesus came to seek the lost. But the next time I preached this and read both Bock and Marshall, I learned that the evidence for this view, which portrays the shepherds as thieves, comes from rabbinic writings in the fifth century![22] Bock concludes: "Thus, the presence of the shepherds is not a negative point. Rather, they picture the lowly and humble who respond to God's message."[23] Lowly and humble, yes! Dishonest and unscrupulous, no!

Besides Bock and Marshall, Joel Green's volume in the NICNT series is worth consulting. On some passages, he provides even more insight into Jewish or Greco-Roman background than Bock or Marshall. Joseph Fitzmyer's volumes in the Anchor Bible series are an outstanding piece of work. But pay attention to how Bock occasionally updates or corrects him. Robert Stein's volume in the NAC series is also useful.

John

For the Gospel of John, three commentaries stand at the head of the class. D. A. Carson's volume in the Pillar New Testament Commentary series is a masterpiece of learning. It is strong not only in exposing the theology communicated by the fourth Gospel, but also it handles the Jewish background quite well. Gary Burge's volume in the NIV Application Commentary is equally outstanding, especially in helping preachers understand how Jesus used the various festivals in Judaism to make statements about himself and his ministry. Both Burge and Carson clued me in to the way Jesus used the imagery associated with the Feast of Tabernacles to proclaim in John 7 that he is the fulfillment of all that the feast anticipated.[24] Burge claims: "It is almost impossible to interpret John 7 without some detailed acquaintance with the Jewish Feast of Tabernacles and how it was celebrated in Jerusalem in the first century." And the "Jewish intertestamental motifs of water and light" shaped the way the ceremonies associated with Tabernacles.[25] This is not surprising given that daylight was becoming shorter and water was becoming scarce due to the lack of rain. Carson provides more detail:

> On the seven days of the Feast, a golden flagon was filled with water from the pool of Siloam and was carried in a procession led by the High Priest back to the temple. As the procession approached the watergate on the south side of the inner court three blasts from the *sopar*—a trumpet connected with joyful occasions—were sounded. While the pilgrims watched, the priests processed around the altar with

the flagon. . . . The water was offered to God at the time of the morning sacrifice, along with the daily drink-offering (of wine). The wine and water were poured into their respective silver bowls, and then poured out before the LORD. . . . Pouring at the Feast of Tabernacles refers symbolically to the messianic age in which a stream from the sacred rock would flow over the whole earth.[26]

With all of this imagery alive in the minds of the pilgrims, how significant that John's Gospel reports:

On the last and greatest day of the festival, Jesus stood and said in a loud voice, "Let anyone who is thirsty come to me and drink. Whoever believes in me, as Scripture has said, rivers of living water will flow from within them." By this he meant the Spirit, whom those who believed in him were later to receive. Up to that time the Spirit had not been given, since Jesus had not yet been glorified. (John 7:37–39)

All of the themes in the above discussion can be found as well in Craig Keener's massive two-volume work, *The Gospel of John: A Commentary*. Keener is well versed in the Old Testament, intertestamental literature, and rabbinic texts—the latter of which he uses with discretion so as not to read later Jewish practices into Judaism at the time of Jesus. There are other good commentaries on the Gospel of John, but you will be hard-pressed to find anything in them that Burge, Carson, and Keener have not already discussed.

3. Read a good work on first-century Judaism.

If those who preach the Gospels look for Old Testament precedents and then use a handful of the most respected commentaries, they will go a long way toward understanding the Jewish and Greco-Roman background to the Gospels and its bearing on an accurate interpretation of the biblical text. But there are two more practices that pastors can pursue. These practices take pastors deeper into the waters of biblical scholarship in which the best commentators wade.

The first of these additional steps is to read a good work or two on first-century Judaism. Craig Blomberg suggested this to me and provided three recommendations. A good place to start is *An Introduction to Early Judaism* by James C. VanderKam. In 217 pages, VanderKam provides a historical survey of Second Temple Judaism, a survey of its literature, and a survey of its leaders, groups, and institutions. A second work is Oskar Skarsaune's *In the Shadow of the Temple: Jewish Influences on Early Christianity*. While quite readable, it tops out at 444 pages, so busy pastors might want to use it more like a dictionary and consult specific sections or chapters as needed. There is hardly a topic that Skarsaune overlooks. He provides more information on the Greco-Roman background than the subtitle of his book suggests. A third volume sheds light on rabbinic Judaism and its development in the first five centuries A.D.—the same time frame in which Christianity began. This 188-page volume (before the notes and indices) is *Judaism when Christianity Began: A Survey of Belief and Practice* by Jacob Neusner, an esteemed yet sometimes controversial expert in rabbinic Judaism.

Furthermore, Craig Keener has included in his John commentary a fine excursus, "The Value of Rabbinic Texts for Johannine Study," which I highly recommend reading before working through Neusner's volume.[27] The reason is twofold. First, it offers a concise (10 pp.), sensible, evangelical approach to using rabbinical sources. Second, it devotes four pages to critiquing

Neusner's "minimalist" approach. Neusner is cautious, perhaps overly so, about using even the Mishnah to understand the time of Jesus. Neusner has been widely criticized by rabbinic scholars who believe in more continuity between later rabbinic Judaism and Judaism in the time of Jesus. As Craig Blomberg quipped, "Orthodox rabbis who are unconvinced that their rabbinic tradition does not go back to the first century or earlier view Jacob Neusner the way evangelicals view Bart Ehrman!"[28]

At this point, I should say something about Alfred Edersheim's classic *The Life and Times of Jesus the Messiah*. When I started preaching a quarter of a century ago, Edersheim's volume was my go-to source for historical-cultural backgrounds for the Gospels. However, as noted already in Ben Witherington's comments, Edersheim is not a reliable source. Whatever good insights he may have are tarnished by his indiscriminate use of rabbinical writings from the first through tenth centuries A.D. to understand what Jesus said and did.[29] Our understanding of rabbinical sources has grown significantly since 1886, when Edersheim's third edition of his book was published.

Some may ask about Kenneth E. Bailey's work on Luke's parables and his recent tome *Jesus through Middle Eastern Eyes: Cultural Studies in the Gospels*. This fine volume received endorsements from several respected New Testament scholars. Bailey comes at his insights from a slightly different perspective. Though he is well versed in a wide array of Jewish literature and the literature of the Eastern Semitic-speaking churches, he is noted for insight that grows out of living for sixty years in the Middle East and observing the life of Bedouin shepherds. His analysis depends in part on similarities between modern Bedouin life and peasant life in rural Israel. While Bailey's insights are helpful in correcting our Western perspective, pastors must always be aware that his cultural anthropology runs the risk of anachronism—reading twentieth-century practices back into the first century.

Overall, my suggestion is to read VanderKam and Keener's excursus first. Have Skarsaune handy to fill in any gaps. As David Turner has observed, "We need to realize the diverse groups that composed the Judaism of Jesus' day."[30] At some point, read Neusner if you want to gain more expertise in rabbinic Judaism in the five centuries after Christ. With respect for all that Edersheim has done, do not bother consulting him.

4. Read the primary sources.

For those pastors who want to take the time, a final practice is to read the primary sources themselves. This is a wonderful venture. To pastors who claim they are too busy for this, I say, "You do not have time to read everything, but you have time to read something." If nothing else, look up the citations you find in the commentaries and read them for yourself in context. This may add no more than ten or fifteen minutes to one's sermon preparation. The other alternative is to do some more extended, systematic reading of the primary sources themselves.

There are five primary sources for understanding the world in which the life and ministry of Jesus took place: (1) the Apocrypha, (2) the Pseudepigrapha, (3) the Dead Sea Scrolls, (4) the Jewish writers Josephus and Philo, and (5) the Mishnah. Before exploring these, you may want to consult an introduction. James C. VanderKam's chapter on "Jewish Literature of the Second Temple Period" in his previously mentioned volume *An Introduction to Early Judaism* is outstanding. My favorite book-length treatment is *Exploring Jewish Literature of the Second*

Temple Period: A Guide for New Testament Students by Larry R. Helyer. I worked through most of it a few years ago between Christmas and New Year's Day. The amount of literature you can read in these five categories is astounding, but Helyer helps to break it down into useful synopses.

The Apocrypha

The place to begin is the Apocrypha. This collection, labeled "hidden things" or "hidden books," *apocrypha* in Greek, consists of fourteen to sixteen books or parts of books that date mostly to the three centuries prior to Christ.[31] Perhaps the most accessible English translation for reading the Apocrypha is the New Revised Standard Version (NRSV). Recently, while I was studying Jesus' challenge to a potential disciple to "let the dead bury their own dead" in Luke 9:60, the Apocrypha helped me understand how the culture would have shaped this potential disciple's plea to bury his father before following Jesus.[32] Sirach 38:16 (also called Ecclesiasticus) offers this piece of proverbial wisdom:

> My child, let your tears fall for the dead,
>   and as one in great pain begin the lament.
> Lay out the body with due ceremony,
>   and do not neglect the burial. (NRSV)

Similarly Tobit 4:3–4 records the counsel that Tobit offers to his son Tobias:

> Then he called his son Tobias, and when he came to him he said, "My son, when I die, give me a proper burial. Honor your mother and do not abandon her all the days of her life. Do whatever pleases her, and do not grieve her in anything. Remember her, my son, because she faced many dangers for

you while you were in her womb. And when she dies, bury her beside me in the same grave." (NRSV)

While the value of burying one's deceased relatives was a priority in the Old Testament (see 1 Kings 19:19–21), references like these give a preacher confidence to say, "During the time of Jesus, burying a family member was a very high priority."

Reading the Apocrypha has also shed light for me on how the development of the wisdom traditions during the intertestamental period influenced the way Jesus taught and presented himself as a sage. For example, when Jesus says, "Give to the one who asks you, and do not turn away from the one who wants to borrow from you" (Matt. 5:42), he reflects not only the teaching of Proverbs but also of Sirach 4:4–5:

> Do not reject a suppliant in distress,
>   or turn your face away from the poor.
> Do not avert your eye from the needy,
>   and give no one reason to curse you. (NRSV)

The Apocrypha, then, sheds light both on Jesus' teaching—particularly the way Jesus presented himself as a Jewish prophetic sage, as Ben Sira (in Sirach) and Pseudo-Solomon (in Wisdom of Solomon) did shortly before him.[33]

The Pseudepigrapha

Along with the Apocrypha, the Pseudepigrapha can help pastors understand the world in which Jesus served and taught. The Greek term *pseudepigrapha* literally means "falsely ascribed" and "designates the Jewish literature written between 200 B.C. and A.D. 200 and spuriously ascribed to various prophets, kings, and ancient worthies mentioned in the Hebrew Scriptures."[34]

Like the Apocrypha, the Pseudepigrapha is a mixture of narrative fiction, hymns (psalms), wisdom, and apocalyptic. To access this material, pastors need to invest in *The Old Testament Pseudepigrapha*, the massive two-volume edition edited by James H. Charlesworth.[35] I will never forget how *2 Baruch* 29 opened up my eyes to what Jesus was doing and saying in John 6.[36] Jesus' miraculous provision of food for five thousand people around the time of Passover and his subsequent claim to be "the bread of life" would have signaled the arrival of the Messiah. *Second Baruch* 29, a text dating to about A.D. 100, describes the condition on the whole earth when the Messiah, the Anointed One, is revealed. Food will be so plentiful that "those who are hungry will enjoy themselves, and they will, moreover, see marvels every day" (*2 Bar.* 29:6). Even more striking is this description: "And it will happen at that time that the treasury of manna will come down again from on high, and they will eat of it in those years because these are they who will have arrived at the consummation of time" (*2 Bar.* 29:8).

Equally stunning is the statement in the *Testament of Joseph* 19:8 (from the *Testaments of the Twelve Patriarchs*) describing what the patriarch saw in a dream: "And I saw that a virgin was born from Judah, wearing a linen stole; and from her was born a spotless lamb." Similarly, the *Testament of Benjamin* 3:8 records words that Jacob allegedly spoke to Joseph, Benjamin's brother:

> Through you will be fulfilled the heavenly prophecy concerning the Lamb of God, the Savior of the world, because the unspotted one will be betrayed by lawless men, and the sinless one will die for impious men by the blood of the covenant for the salvation of the gentiles and of Israel and the destruction of Beliar and his servants.

Surely this provides some context for the great exclamation by John the Baptist the first time he saw Jesus: "Look, the Lamb of God who takes away the sin of the world!" (John 1:29). Based on these references, D. A. Carson concludes that John "probably had in mind the apocalyptic lamb, the warrior lamb, found in some Jewish texts"—the two in the *Testaments of the Twelve Patriarchs* as well as in *1 Enoch* 90:9–12.[37]

The Dead Sea Scrolls

In addition to the Apocrypha and Pseudepigrapha, the Dead Sea Scrolls offer us a window into Jewish thought and practice during the time of Jesus. Approximately three-quarters of the scrolls found near Qumran and at other sites along the Dead Sea are nonbiblical texts.[38] These nonbiblical texts can be divided into *sectarian* and *nonsectarian* writings.[39] The former term refers to those writings—about 40 percent of the nonbiblical texts—that appear to be the central documents of the group or groups responsible for the Dead Sea Scrolls.[40] The other 60 percent of these nonbiblical texts reflect the various streams of Judaism within Palestine at the time.

The most affordable, accessible edition for pastors is *A New Translation: The Dead Sea Scrolls* by Michael Wise, Martin Abegg, Jr., and Edward Cook. It is the most recent English translation available, revised in 2005. *The Complete Dead Sea Scrolls in English* by Geza Vermes is also a fine translation and affordable. The most recent edition was published in 1995. The other major English edition is the two-volume work by Florentino García Martínez and W. G. E. Watson, *The Dead Sea Scrolls Translated: The Qumran Texts in English*, published in 1997. Although the edition by Wise, Abegg, and Cook is my personal preference, any edition will suffice. When I asked Weston W. Fields, executive director of the Dead Sea Scrolls Foundation in Jerusalem, which edition he recommends, he replied that he uses all three and suggests the use of all three—especially since none of the editions is entirely complete.[41]

Since the material in the Dead Sea Scrolls seems a bit exotic to modern readers, and since its preservation is fragmentary, pastors may find it helpful to read a good introduction. The chapter in Larry Helyer's *Exploring Jewish Literature of the Second Temple Period* will be sufficient for most. Another fine treatment is *The Dead Sea Scrolls Today* (now in its second edition) by James C. VanderKam. For an even more comprehensive discussion, consult *The Meaning of the Dead Sea Scrolls* by James VanderKam and Peter Flint.

So what is the payoff for reading the Dead Sea Scrolls when it comes to understanding the Gospels? Larry Helyer cites several parallels between the Qumran texts and the New Testament—all of which apply to the Gospels. These include: a manner of reading Old Testament Scripture as pointing to a messiah, a high standard of morality and ethics, and the conviction that the new covenant prophesied by Jeremiah had been established between God and a repentant remnant.[42] Jesus' criticism of the Pharisees finds parallels in the community's criticism of their opponents.[43]

Recently my reading of the Dead Sea Scrolls helped me understand the force of Jesus' words in Luke 18:22 to the rich ruler who wanted to know what he must do to inherit eternal life. When the ruler claimed that he had kept the Ten Commandments from childhood, Jesus exposed this ruler's heart with these words: "You still lack one thing. Sell everything you have and give to the poor, and you will have treasure in heaven. Then come, follow me." What struck me was both the correspondence and contrast between this mandate and the one given in the *Community Rule* scroll (also known as *Charter of a Jewish Sectarian Association*). Two passages, 1:11–13 and 6:19–22, make it clear that a man who joined the community had to turn over his property to the community. Jesus' mandate, then, had some cultural precedence. Yet Jesus instructed the young man to give money to the poor rather than to the community founded by Jesus! This highlights Jesus' concern for the poor as well as Jesus' immunity to greed. This is not to say that the community behind the Dead Sea Scrolls was motivated by greed. Yet even with cultural precedent for asking the ruler to give his wealth to Jesus' community to display loyalty to God, Jesus instead instructs the man to give his wealth elsewhere.

Philo and Josephus

A fourth primary source for understanding the New Testament Gospels consists of the Jewish writers Philo (ca. 20 B.C.–A.D. 50) and Flavius Josephus (ca. A.D. 37–100). Philo, from Alexandria, Egypt, offers us a "glimpse into the world of highly educated Jews quite at home in the Hellenistic culture at the end of the first century B.C. and in the first half of the first century A.D." And Josephus was "a Jewish historian who wrote for a cultured Roman audience."[44] Both his *Jewish War* and *Antiquities of the Jews* provide much information about thought and life during the time of Jesus. While the Loeb Classical Library volumes are the choice of scholars, especially since they include the Greek text and an English translation on facing pages, one-volume works make more sense for most pastors.[45] For Philo, consult *The Works of Philo: Complete and Unabridged*, translated by C. D. Yonge. For Josephus, get a copy of *The Works of Josephus: Complete and Unabridged*, translated by William Whiston.

With all the time demands on pastors, it is fair to ask if reading Philo and Josephus is necessary. Certainly it is not absolutely essential. Good commentaries on the Gospels can point out their insights. But having these volumes available will allow a pastor to read a citation or check a quotation in its context. What pastor preaching on the opening verses of John would not profit from reading Philo's discussion of the Logos or Word of God?[46] What pastor preaching on Matthew 2 and the story of Jesus' birth would not profit from reading Josephus' material on Herod?[47] After reading Josephus' descriptions of Herod, I was able to paint this picture of Herod in a sermon on Matthew 2:16–18:

> Herod was not the kind of king you'd want to engage in conversation. And it's not just because Herod had bad breath, as Jewish historian Josephus reveals. It's because he was a brutal tyrant. Anyone who threatened his throne ended up in a morgue. When he threw a poolside party at his palace, he hired a thug to dunk his brother-in-law in the swimming pool and hold him under until he drowned. He had his wife executed. He executed her brother. He executed two sons who were more interested in ruling than Herod thought they should be. And five days before his own death, when Herod was so sick that he couldn't get out of bed, he ordered the execution of his son, Antipater, who was telling people that he would probably take over as king when his old man died.

This certainly enlightens our understanding when we read in Matthew 2:3 that King Herod was "disturbed, and all Jerusalem with him" when some magi came asking where they could find the one who had been born king of the Jews.

The Mishnah

A final primary source for understanding the world in which the life and ministry of Jesus took place is the Mishnah. The Mishnah is "an elaborate casebook of religious law, custom, and tradition" written down about A.D. 200 but consisting of contributions from some 150 rabbis whose lives spanned a range from approximately 50 B.C. to A.D. 200.[48] Jacob Neusner describes it as "a six-part code of descriptive rules formulated toward the end of the second century A.D. by a small number of Jewish sages and put forth as the constitution of Judaism under the sponsorship of Judah the Patriarch, the head of the Jewish community of Palestine at the end of that century."[49] Purportedly "Moses received Torah in two media, in writing and in memory, the memorized part of the Torah being received and handed on in a process of oral formulation and oral transmission."[50] The Mishnah contains this "Oral Torah" that was acquired and transmitted and eventually written down by the rabbis.[51]

The Mishnah can offer insights into Judaism during the time of Jesus when used judiciously. D. A. Carson explains: "The Mishnah (ca. A.D. 200) cannot be read back into A.D. 30 as if Judaism had not faced the growth of Christianity and the shattering destruction of temple and cultus. Nevertheless it preserves more traditional material than is sometimes thought."[52] Once again, consulting the most reputable commentators is wise in order to gauge whether or not a particular passage from the Mishnah sheds light on a particular text in the Gospels or rather reflects Judaism after the destruction of the temple in A.D. 70.

The standard edition is *The Mishnah: A New Translation* by Jacob Neusner. It is a valuable addition to a pastor's library, although pastors will most likely refer to it selectively as cited in commentaries as opposed to reading through it. Herbert

Danby's translation, *The Mishnah*, first published in 1933, is still reliable.[53]

Larry Helyer is certainly right when he says: "Only a highly motivated reader, with a deep commitment to traditional or Orthodox Judaism, will likely plod through this mass of material, especially without teacher or fellow traveler."[54] At first, pastors unfamiliar with the Mishnah may miss the references to it in the standard commentaries on the Gospels. Typically, though, the citations of the Mishnah in these commentaries use the abbreviation *m.* before the particular tractate—a subdivision in one of the six "orders" or "divisions"—being cited. So a citation like *m. Shabb.* 7.2 refers to chapter 7, section 2 of the Mishnah tractate *Shabbat*.

I found the Mishnah tractate *Shabbat* quite helpful when preaching on John 5. In John 5 Jesus receives persecution and prosecution for allegedly breaking the Sabbath by healing a disabled man and instructing him to pick up his mat and walk. The commentaries I used referred me to *Shabbat* 7:2, which lists thirty-nine categories of labor prohibited by the rabbis on the Sabbath. This list gives insight into the "fence around the law" that would help Jewish people refrain from breaking the Sabbath. The list prohibits items such as sewing two stitches, trapping a deer, writing two letters, erasing two letters, putting out a fire, and kindling a fire. The thirty-ninth item prohibits the transportation of an object from one domain to another. This explains why the religious leaders could say to the healed man that "the law forbids you to carry your mat" (John 5:10).

Similarly, a pastor who preaches on Luke 4:16–30, the account of Jesus preaching in the synagogue in Nazareth, will profit from reading chapter 4 in the Mishnah tractate *Megillah*. This chapter sheds light on how Scripture readings were to be done in a synagogue setting. Jesus' act of standing and reading a brief portion from the prophet Isaiah fits with what the Mishnah says about readings from the Torah and the prophets. Even Jesus' interjection of language from Isaiah 58:6 toward the end of his reading of Isaiah 61:1–2 (see Luke 4:18) fits into the instruction that the readers may skip from place to place in the prophetic lections but not in the Torah lections. Darrell Bock affirms the use of the Mishnah for understanding the synagogue since "synagogue tradition as liturgy was likely to have been conservative in its development and because the synagogue was an old institution by this point [when the Mishnah was written]."[55]

If all of this seems like a lot of work, well, it is! But it is worth it when we consider what is at stake. As D. A. Carson says, "We are dealing with God's thoughts: we are obligated to take the greatest pains to understand them truly and to explain them clearly."[56] The words and works of Jesus Christ happened in a specific historical-cultural context—the world of Second Temple Judaism in first-century Palestine. Understanding what Jesus said and did requires us to understand this context. So, at the very least, those who preach the Gospels should pay attention to any Old Testament precedents and should consult a handful of the most respected commentaries. Those who want to dig deeper will profit from reading a work or two on first-century Judaism and reading the primary sources themselves. Our Lord and our listeners deserve this kind of effort from those who stand up to preach the Gospels.

4

CONFLICTING REPORTS?

When parallel accounts seem contradictory

Recently while preparing a sermon on Luke 9:28–36, a detail in Luke's account caught me off guard. The Evangelist has just reported a stunning prediction by Jesus: "Truly I tell you, some who are standing here will not taste death before they see the kingdom of God" (v. 27). Then Luke reports: "About eight days after Jesus said this, he took Peter, John and James with him and went up onto a mountain to pray" (v. 28). What caught me off guard was Luke's reference to "about eight days." The parallel passage in Mark 9:2 reads: "After six days Jesus took Peter, James and John with him and led them up a high mountain, where they were all alone." The parallel account in Matthew 17:1 also reads "after six days."

So why the apparent discrepancy? As I pondered the matter, the little word *about* in Luke's account elicited a sigh of relief. Luke is clearly estimating, while Matthew and Mark are giving precise time measurements. Nothing wrong with that. But given Luke's meticulous research (1:1–4), why would he settle for an estimate when he could have provided a precise measurement of time? After all, there is an overwhelming consensus that the Gospels of Matthew and Mark appeared prior to Luke's Gospel.

So why make a deliberate change from a precise measurement of time to an estimate? Furthermore, why does Luke add the infinitive *to pray*, which Matthew and Mark both lack? The infinitive undoubtedly expresses the purpose for their trek. Why did Matthew and Mark not see fit to include this?

Before exploring the reason for these editorial changes, we should note that this is not an isolated example. When preachers compare a particular preaching text in the Gospels with its parallel accounts, they will discover various editorial differences between the accounts.[1] As noted in the above examples, a gospel writer may omit what another writer includes or may include a detail that another writer omits. Or a gospel writer may alter a detail—without compromising the integrity of the account as Luke does when changing Mark's "six days" to "about eight days." Sometimes a gospel writer has transposed an account, moving what is found in one location in one Synoptic Gospel to a different setting in another Gospel. For example, New Testament scholar Scot McKnight notes that "Jesus' compassion for Jerusalem is found at the end of the woes in Matthew (23:37–39), but occurs in a completely different context in Luke (13:34–35)."[2] Furthermore, one gospel writer may offer an explanation that another gospel lacks. For example, in the account where the Pharisees criticize Jesus' disciples for not washing their hands before they eat, Mark alone explains the practice (7:3–4) while Matthew and Luke offer no such explanation.

How Redaction Criticism Can Help Preachers

To determine the purpose behind the editorial changes from one parallel account to another, a wise preacher will turn to the discipline of redaction criticism. Grant Osborne explains:

Redaction criticism is a historical and literary discipline which studies both the way the redactors/editors/authors changed their sources and the seams or transitions they utilized to link those traditions into a unified whole. The purpose of this approach is to recover the author's theology and setting.[3]

Unfortunately redaction criticism emerged in a climate that was skeptical, if not hostile, to the historicity of the Gospels. This means that evangelical preachers must redeem it from the radical antihistorical presuppositions with which it was originally practiced. Redaction criticism developed out of two previous schools of criticism—*form* criticism and its stepchild *source* criticism.[4] Form criticism, which originated in post-World War I Germany, attempted to uncover the underlying oral traditions that were transmitted in given forms and used in a specific *Sitz im Leben* (setting in life) in the church. While form criticism helped readers identify different kinds of "forms"—such as pronouncement stories or miracle stories—used to communicate ideas, it assumed that the church created or developed these forms to meet its needs. That is, the church put words in Jesus' mouth that he did not necessarily say. *Source* or *tradition* criticism took this a step further by attempting to reconstruct the history or development of gospel traditions from the earliest sources to the final form. This led to redaction criticism, a discipline pioneered by three scholars in post-World War II Germany—Günther Bornkamm, Hans Conzelmann, and Willi Marxsen. These redaction critics attempted to answer why a particular gospel writer changed another Gospel's account of a saying or deed of Jesus. In the process, they assumed an antithesis between history and theology.

D. A. Carson castigates such a radical perspective: "It is methodologically irresponsible to pit history against theology as if the two could not be compatible." He explains: "It is illegitimate to reject *a priori* as unhistorical all that is abnormal, the more so if the context has prompted the reader to expect the abnormal."[5] Furthermore, he wonders why we must assume that the most influential mind in the history of the world—Jesus—was incapable of the complex thoughts or development of themes that are freely credited to his followers.[6]

An evangelical preacher, then, will practice redaction criticism with the assumption that the various gospel writers "were given the freedom by God to omit, expand and highlight these traditions in order to bring out individual nuances peculiar to their own gospel."[7] This is similar to what modern historians have done with the historical sources related to America's sixteenth president, Abraham Lincoln. I recently read two books that use the historical sources about Lincoln to argue two different points. In *Team of Rivals: The Political Genius of Abraham Lincoln*, Doris Kearns Goodwin argues that Lincoln demonstrated political genius by appointing his eminent rivals to his cabinet.[8] This enabled him to steer the country through its darkest days. Goodwin never distorts the facts. She simply selects some, omits others, and arranges what she selects to make her case. Working from the same historical materials, Douglas L. Wilson argues another point. In his book *Lincoln's Sword: The Presidency and the Power of Words*, Wilson makes the case that Lincoln's literary talent as a writer was a telling factor in his successes as president.[9]

Here is a case, then, of two accounts that make different arguments working from the same historical materials. Doris Kearns Goodwin traces Lincoln's success to his ability to bring political rivals into his team. Douglas L. Wilson traces Lincoln's success to his ability to use words to shape public opinion and public policy. Which is correct? Both. In fact, the inside flap of the cover of Wilson's book contains this plug from Goodwin: "This book is so good that it will shape Lincoln scholarship for generations." Clearly these writers see their work with their differing emphases as compatible. This is the case with the New Testament Gospels.

Before looking at some specific examples, two clarifications offered by D. A. Carson are worth considering. Both have to do with not exaggerating the differences between gospel accounts. First, Carson observes that "whatever else Jesus was, He was an itinerant preacher. As anyone who has done much itinerant preaching knows, minor variations of the same messages or re-arrangements of them come out again and again."[10] Here it is helpful to recognize the gospel writers' practice of paraphrase.[11] As Craig L. Blomberg notes, "Even defenders of Scripture's infallibility freely admit that the Evangelists usually record only Jesus' *ipsissima vox* (actual voice) rather than his *ipsissima verba* (actual words)."[12] A second clarification noted by Carson is that the differences between parallel accounts "*may* be prompted by purely theological considerations, but equally they *may* be prompted by stylistic concerns or even by additional information springing from further research (Luke 1:1–4)."[13] The lesson is clear: we must not overread these texts by finding a significant theological emphasis behind every minor variation between accounts. We dare not see a castle where the gospel writer has built only a shed.

Rich Discoveries

So what should preachers expect to find as they observe the differences between a gospel text they choose to preach and its parallel accounts? Here are a few examples of the rich discoveries preachers will make.

First, let me return to the example cited at the beginning of this chapter. In my sermon preparation on Luke 9:28–36, I wrestled with Luke's reference to "about eight days later" (v. 28) when Mark (9:2) and Matthew (17:1)—both earlier Gospels—specified "six days later." The best explanation I found was that Luke has altered the time reference to cast this event as a "sacred assembly" that took place on the eighth day of the Feast of Booths (see Lev. 23:36). New Testament scholar Craig Evans suggests that "Luke has taken the raw materials that he found in the Marcan version of the transfiguration and has enriched the parallels in such a way as to enhance the presentation of Jesus as God's Son (and Servant) whose authority and significance greatly surpass those of Moses and Elijah."[14] As Evans observes, "Undoubtedly, in the evangelist's mind there could be no holier convocation than the meeting of Moses, Elijah, and Jesus; God's Law-giver, Prophet, and Son."[15] Furthermore, Luke's addition of the infinitive *to pray*—an element not found in Mark's or Matthew's account—reflects Luke's concern to portray Jesus as a person of prayer.[16]

Second, a preacher studying for a message on Luke 4:14–30—Jesus' homecoming and teaching at Nazareth—will observe that "Luke has deliberately brought forward the story to this point."[17] I. Howard Marshall observes that in both Mark (6:1–6) and Matthew (13:53–58), "a similar story appears at a considerably later state, and internal features in the present story (4:23) suggest that it is not in its original position."[18] How do we account, then, for Luke beginning the story of Jesus' ministry in Galilee with a story that happened later? This is similar to a Civil War historian's decision to begin the story of this war—which occurred from 1861 to 1865—with the account Lincoln's delivery of the Gettysburg Address in 1863. Marshall argues that the narrative is placed at the beginning of Luke's account for its "programmatic significance" as it contains many of Luke's themes in a nutshell.[19]

As noted in the previous two examples, consultation with the major commentators is helpful. Preachers will want to wrestle on their own with the question as to why a particular gospel writer included or left out details a parallel gospel account did not. But after making a tentative suggestion, wise pastors will consult the works of others who have devoted hours of thought to these issues.

Another account for which redaction criticism provides significant help for preachers is the "storm story" recorded in Matthew 8:23–27, Mark 4:35–41, and Luke 8:22–25. My first experience with preaching this story came in a series on the Gospel of Mark. The first time I preached it, I grouped it with the three miracle stories in Mark 5 and ended up preaching Mark 4:35–5:43. My preaching idea was that *Jesus possesses absolute power over the most powerful forces in the universe.* Essentially the miracles recorded in these chapters demonstrate Jesus' power over the forces of nature (4:35–41), over evil spiritual forces (5:1–20), and over sickness and death (5:21–43). Now I am not embarrassed by this sermon. Unlike some that I have preached two decades ago, I have not relegated it to a file called "Sermons I Wish I Never Preached." However, when I returned to this text a decade later, a more careful comparison with the parallel accounts led me in a slightly different direction.

As I preached through Mark's Gospel for a second time to a different congregation, I noticed how Mark's placement of the storm story differs from Matthew's and Luke's. Matthew records it in the middle of an anthology of Jesus' works of power.[20] Within the middle of this anthology, it stands as the first of three miracle stories that are grouped geographically (around the crossing of the Sea of Galilee) and theologically (around the unparalleled authority displayed by Jesus).[21] Luke's placement reflects Mark's more closely as the storm story follows a section of Jesus' parables—all of which center on the Word of God. However, Luke does not attempt to make a tight connection between the parables and the storm story. He simply begins with a general temporal reference: "Now it happened on one of those days" (8:22).[22] Mark's account is unique. He opens his account with a specific temporal reference: "That day when evening came" (4:35). Mark, then, has deliberately timed his account to correspond to the day when Jesus taught his parables,[23] including two parables of the kingdom that occur just prior to the storm story (see Mark 4:26–34).

When I observed Mark's emphasis on the storm story happening later on a day when Jesus had taught in parables that the kingdom of God would grow despite its small beginnings, I saw an emphasis I had previously missed. So instead of including the storm story with the miracle stories in Mark 5, I opted to preach Mark 4:35–41 by itself and focus on its relationship to the kingdom parables immediately before it. Early in my sermon, I said:

> "That day when evening came." Jesus had drilled it into the minds of his followers that the kingdom he was announcing, the kingdom of God, depended on God. God is going to grow his kingdom. God is going to make it happen. Now, a little bit later in the day, God has decided that it is test time. Will Jesus' followers have this confidence in God's kingdom when it looks like they, along with the leader of this kingdom, might wind up dead in the Sea of Galilee?

Then, as the sermon developed, I pointed out how the disciples were concerned with much more than physical safety in the midst of the storm, when they said to Jesus: "Teacher, don't you care if we drown?" (Mark 4:38). I said to my listeners:

This storm has caused the disciples to doubt the certainty of God's promise. Remember, they have kingdom fever! They had turned their backs on their careers and had broken family ties to follow Jesus. The panic that hit them in that boat was more than the fear of losing their lives. This swirl of emotions emerged from a deeper fear. It was the fear that the cause for which they had given their lives was going to sink. It was the fear that Jesus would never be king over this great kingdom, God's kingdom. It was a fear that they had given their lives to a lost cause.

Eventually, I arrived at my preaching idea: *you can be sure that the kingdom to which you have given your life will succeed because the King has unlimited power.* This idea certainly reflected the main point of my sermon a decade before when I emphasized that *Jesus possesses unlimited power over the most powerful forces of the universe.* But it also took into consideration the unique way Mark linked the storm story with Jesus' teaching a few hours prior to the storm. Without violating any facts, Mark highlighted details that made this legitimate link when the other gospel writers chose not to do so.

Now let me repeat: preachers must not find a castle where the gospel writer intended only to build a shed. But preachers who pay attention to the differences between parallel accounts will enrich their preaching in the Gospels as they discover and communicate the unique emphases of a particular gospel writer's telling of the account.

How to Practice Redaction Criticism

How, then, do evangelical preachers practice redaction criticism in a responsible way? How do preachers discover the unique emphases of the gospel writers—emphases that often get overlooked? Fortunately there are some approaches, as well as tools for these approaches, to help preachers in their study of parallel accounts. As with other steps in the exegetical process, preachers will do well to do their own work first. Then, after the *independent study* phase, preachers should enter the *resource phase* and consult the thinking of others.

Independent Study Phase

The independent study phase involves comparing the parallel accounts. This seems relatively simple, but it is not always as easy as it seems. For this phase of the process, a preacher will need to invest in a good synopsis. A synopsis places parallel accounts of the same event or teaching of Jesus in side-by-side columns. This is a bit different than a "harmony" that attempts to construct a life of Jesus.[24] A "harmony" may have an apologetic aim, seeking to establish the truthfulness of an event or events in the life of Jesus.[25] But the purpose of a synopsis is to enable the reader to compare the similarities in the accounts, both line by line and word by word. The standard edition is the *Synopsis of the Four Gospels* by Kurt Aland. It is available in a Greek edition, an English edition using the Revised Standard Version, and a Greek-English edition.[26] Some Bible software programs also provide a synopsis. Currently an edition of Aland's *Synopsis* is available for Logos Bible Software, and BibleWorks contains a "Synopsis Window" feature that allows users to display parallel passages in parallel columns.

But how does a preacher make use of a synopsis? First, do a big-picture scan, which is simply a quick visual scan of the columns in a parallel account to note the obvious differences. For example, suppose I am preaching on Matthew 12:1–14. In Aland's *Synopsis*, this text includes two units: "Plucking Grain on the Sabbath" and "The Man with the Withered Hand." I will use only the former unit (12:1–8) as an example. In a minute or so, I can make four observations:

1. The account appears in all three Synoptic Gospels.
2. The account follows the same general flow in all three Gospels.
3. Matthew includes a significant statement by Jesus (vv. 5–7) that the others do not have.
4. All three accounts conclude with the same saying by Jesus ("The Son of Man is Lord of the Sabbath").

Of these four observations, the third is the most notable. According to Matthew's account, after Jesus used the example of David eating "the bread of the Presence," he cites another example before moving to the ending pronouncement about the Son of Man being Lord of the Sabbath. Mark and Luke move right from the David example to the "Lord of the Sabbath" saying. The additional example that Matthew includes is:

Or haven't you read in the Law that the priests on Sabbath duty in the temple desecrate the Sabbath and yet are innocent? I tell you that something greater than the temple is here. If you had known what these words mean, "I desire mercy, not sacrifice," you would not have condemned the innocent. (Matt. 12:5–7)

Now after performing a big-picture scan, a preacher may decide to perform a more detailed analysis. Preachers must decide how much time they can devote to such an analysis and how much of the text they should analyze. Before describing the process, let me say that I sometimes perform a more detailed analysis, but not always. There are occasions when I will devote the time to another aspect of exegesis that seems more urgent. For example, I may decide in this text to do some historical-culture research on how the Pharisees, as well as the mainstream population, observed the Sabbath in Jesus' day. This means reading some "Second Temple" texts as well as appropriate sections on the Sabbath in the Mishnah.[27] Even a pastor who spends fifteen to twenty-five hours preparing a sermon cannot uncover every stone. Frankly, the detailed analysis of parallel accounts takes time.

The detailed analysis I am proposing involves underlining a synopsis. I first learned this technique from Scot McKnight's book *Interpreting the Synoptic Gospels*, more than two decades ago. Basically the process consists of underlining words and phrases with colored pencils to show similarities and differences between the synoptic accounts. In some cases, a reader may wish to underline every word of every line in a particular section. At other times, a reader might want to be selective so that the process does not become too tedious. I have slightly adapted McKnight's color scheme, using various colors to represent the way in which a particular word is parallel (or not) with what appears in a parallel account:[28]

- Unparalleled (not found in either of the other Gospels)—Purple
- All three Synoptics ("triple tradition")—Blue

- Same in Matthew and Mark (but not in Luke)—Yellow
- Same in Mark and Luke (but not in Matthew)—Green
- Same in Matthew and Luke (but not in Mark)—Red

At this level of detail, it is best to work with the Greek text. However, I have underlined enough events or sayings in both a Greek synopsis and an English synopsis to know that there is definite value for those who can work only with an English synopsis.

Exactly what does a detailed study yield when underlining Matthew 12:1–8 and the parallel accounts in Mark 2:23–28 and Luke 6:1–5? While I made no earth-shaking discoveries, I noted that Matthew begins with a different temporal reference than the other two Synoptics. His account begins with "At that time," whereas Mark and Luke begin by noting that this event happened on a Sabbath. Matthew alone notes the motive for plucking grain on the Sabbath, adding the detail that Jesus' disciples "were hungry" (12:1). Furthermore, both Matthew and Luke note that the disciples ate the heads of grain they picked, while Mark does not include this detail. Then Matthew and Luke both highlight the Pharisees' surprise or objection to this action by including the interjection "look" at the beginning of their protest to Jesus (Matt. 12:2; Mark 2:24). Luke does not include this detail. Finally, I noted that Matthew alone includes the conjunction *for* (*gar*) before Jesus' final statement about the Son of Man being Lord of the Sabbath (v. 8). Jesus, then, introduces his final statement as a ground for the innocence of the disciples (v. 7) and perhaps as a declaration of the Messiah's supremacy over the temple (v. 6).[29] Matthew, then, does not use this event to make a different point from Mark and Luke in their Gospels. Still, the little differences gleaned from underlining can help preachers see the nuances of Matthew in relating this particular conversation in the life of Jesus.

Resource Study Phase

Once preachers have done their independent study, it is time for them to consult the work of others. In some cases, where preachers devote time to other exegetical tasks given the nature of a particular preaching unit, they may move right to this stage. An obvious source of help is the major commentaries. The best ones will discuss how a particular gospel writer's account resembles and differs from the parallel accounts in the other Synoptic Gospels.

One of the most helpful resources is Darrell Bock's *Jesus according to Scripture: Restoring the Portrait from the Gospels*. Bock includes a meaty, yet concise, discussion of every unit in the Synoptic Gospels. He breaks the accounts down into 294 units, and he devotes roughly half a page to two pages for each unit. Even though he has devised his own breakdown and numbering of units, Bock cites the unit number in Aland and a couple of other key synopses for each unit.

Conclusion

A few years ago, an esteemed Old Testament seminar professor shared with our class a humorous story about a preaching blunder he instigated. His exegetical study of Psalm 96 led to the discovery that the psalm was well suited for a sermon on world missions. So he rushed down the hall to the office of the world missions professor to share his discovery. The world missions professor was so moved that he chose Psalm 96 as his sermon text the next time he served as a guest preacher. The Sunday after the world missions professor preached Psalm 96, my Old Testament preacher was scheduled to preach at the same church. Guess what text he chose. Yes, Psalm 96. After the message, an older gentleman found him and scolded him for preaching the same sermon his colleague had preached. The older gentleman then said: "You need to get your act together at your seminary. When one of you preaches a sermon, he needs to make sure to put the sermon notes or manuscript at the bottom of the pile so the next guy who preaches won't use it." Obviously that missed the point. There was a different explanation for two preachers preaching from the same text on back-to-back Sundays.

Similarly we miss the point if we accuse the gospel writers of not getting their stories straight. We miss the point if we think that differences between parallel accounts in the Gospels reflect a lack of unity or consistency or integrity or even a lack of accuracy in the biblical text. The differences between parallel accounts provide preachers with both a responsibility and an opportunity. The responsibility is to avoid the false impression that the accounts are not united—"that different, even contradictory, stories are being told among the Gospels."[30] The opportunity is to bring out the unique aspects of each Gospel. This is necessary because "conservatives tend to merge the accounts so entirely that the themes of the individual books are swallowed up in setting for the combined story."[31] The fact is, the "differences" between the various accounts lead to some of the richest discoveries a preacher will ever make—and preach.

5

DEALING WITH DARKNESS

*Preaching on Jesus' confrontations
with Satan and demons*

Some of the most difficult texts to preach in the gospel accounts are the ones in which Jesus confronts Satan and demons. In a recent message on Luke 8:22–56, I pointed out how Luke puts together stories that highlight Jesus' power over nature, demons, illness, and death. Guess which force baffled my listeners the most. We resonate with Jesus being powerful over nature, illness, and death. But North Americans are not quite sure what to do with a story in which Jesus shows his power over a legion of demons by casting them out of a man who lived among the tombs and sending this legion into a herd of pigs that plunge off a cliff to their death in the Sea of Galilee.[1]

Two factors underlie this difficulty. The first is our culture's tendency toward a naturalistic worldview in which demonic or supernatural forces have little, if any, place. Of course, vampires and witches find their way into popular novels. Likewise, both evil and good supernatural forces take the stage in many movies and video games. Some of these, like the *Star Wars* and *Matrix* sagas, fit into the science fiction genre. Yet gamers who play *Hunted: The Demon's Forge* on an Xbox 360 or Playstation 3 do battle with heinous demonic creatures who emerge from underground.

Even so, discussions of evil in our society—whether about school shootings, serial killings, or molestation—rarely turn to anything demonic as the culprit. Media pundits trace these despicable acts instead to a troubled childhood or an overexposure to violence on television. Mental health professionals diagnose the cause of delusion or an altered state of consciousness as the result of a hallucinogenic drug or a mental illness such as "dissociative identity disorder"—not the result of influence or control by an evil spirit.[2]

A second factor that makes the proclamation of these texts challenging is the nature of spiritual warfare in North America versus the way spiritual warfare presents itself in countries more entrenched in occult practices. The subtle way the Evil One often operates in North America fools some into thinking that spiritual warfare does not really occur here at the level it does elsewhere. Failing to account for Satan's subtlety can blind us to spiritual warfare. As Haddon Robinson once stated in a sermon on temptation from Genesis 3:1–6, "When Satan approaches us, he never comes dragging the chains that will enslave us."[3]

A church I previously served as pastor has a sister-church relationship with a wonderful evangelical congregation in southern Haiti. I traveled there three times in the 1990s and spent considerable time in the church's remote village. We visited sick people, organized youth events, offered a dental clinic, and showed the *Jesus* film at open-air evangelistic events. I preached several times at our sister-church and in several other evangelical congregations in Haiti's southern peninsula. During our visits, we would see voodoo paraphernalia throughout the village, and we would sometimes lie awake at night listening to the pounding of drums at a voodoo ceremony. All of us had a more palpable sense of spiritual darkness than we ever felt in our home community in the United States. Invariably a team member from our American church would remark: "Wow, they really have spiritual warfare here! Now I know what spiritual warfare is really like."

The fact is, we face spiritual warfare in North America just as intensely as Haitians. The difference is in the form it takes. In every place I have lived, I have noticed how the Evil One tries to undermine God's work in my life and the lives of others through the relentless barrage of advertisement that entices us to greed. The battle is no less intense, then, than it is in a culture where Satan's strategy of choice is voodoo rituals and sacrifices. But the subtlety of it all causes us to miss it when it appears. A deficient understanding of spiritual warfare impacts the way we hear the Gospels describe Jesus' conflict with Satan and demons. Such conflicts seem odd and irrelevant to our lives in twenty-first-century America.

What, then, is a preacher to do? Here are three strategies for preaching from texts in the Gospels where Jesus withstands the temptation of Satan and takes on the demonic forces that trouble his people.

Develop a Theology of Spiritual Warfare

The first strategy for preaching texts from the Gospels that narrate Jesus' battle with Satan and his evil forces is to take time in your preaching to develop a theology of spiritual warfare. Admittedly, this might require five to ten minutes of a sermon. But the investment is worth the return. Hearers of Scripture need a theological framework to help them process the message that a particular gospel text is communicating. This is especially important in preaching texts where Jesus casts out demons and instructs the Twelve to do likewise.

What follows is a brief theology of spiritual warfare that I first developed in a graduate course I took.[4] I have frequently worked parts of it into sermons on texts that deal with satanic and demonic themes. This brief theology consists of eight statements.

1. Spiritual warfare is the believer's struggle against everything that sets itself against the knowledge of God (Eph. 6:10–12; 2 Cor. 10:3–5).

2. Three forms of evil influence fight against our commitment to know and love God: the world, the flesh, and the Devil. The world is the unhealthy social environment in which we live, including peer pressure, immoral values, and so on. The flesh refers to our inner tendency to think and to do evil. The Devil is an intelligent, powerful, spirit-being who leads a host of other powerful, evil spirits (Eph. 2:1–3; 1 John 2:15–17; 3:7–10).

3. God is greater than Satan. Jesus triumphed over Satan and his demons by his death on the cross. Satan and his forces are defeated enemies. Though Satan can cause major problems, primarily through deception, accusation, and temptation, God limits what Satan can do (Job 1:6–12; 2:1–7; Eph. 1:19–23; Col. 2:13–15; 1 John 4:4).

4. Our primary weapons that God gives us to access his power in spiritual warfare are truth, righteousness, the gospel of peace, faith, salvation (who we are in Christ), and Scripture. Prayer must accompany the use of these

resources. Prayer is the heart of spiritual warfare, and all prayer is "warfare prayer" (Eph. 6:10–20).

5. Believers should avoid all forms of contact with the demonic, including astrology, horoscopes, demon movies, demon music, demon video and computer games, Ouija, charms, séances, and new age materials (Deut. 18:9–20; Acts 19:18–20).

6. Satan has absolutely no legitimate authority over a believer. When we believe in the Lord Jesus Christ, all sins are forgiven, and all cultic vows, promises, and covenants are broken. Demons have no authority over a believer and have no legal right to invade a believer because of sin or to attach themselves to a believer's soul (Col. 1:13–14; 2:9–15). However, they can wield some level of control over a believer because of a believer's sin (Eph. 4:27). Apparently an evil spirit can empower a believer's tendency to sin (Matt. 16:22–23; Acts 5:3).

7. The primary way for a believer to deal with personal sin is through spiritual disciplines, not deliverance from demons of lust, greed, lying, and so on (Phil. 2:12–13; 1 Tim. 4:7).

8. Believers are not called to engage territorial spirits by praying against them, serving them notice, evicting them, or binding them. While we should certainly pray for God to hinder and stop the activities of territorial spirits in our region or neighborhood, we do not need to identify names of demons, their hierarchy, power points, or "ley lines"[5] for our prayers to be more effective. Our role in tearing down territorial strongholds is to pray fervently and trust our powerful God to deal with these

wicked beings as he wills. (See Daniel's approach in Dan. 10:1–21 and Paul's approach in Acts 13 and 19.)

Recently I worked material from this brief theological summary into a sermon I preached from Luke 4:31–44 titled "Jesus and the Forces of Darkness." I began by admitting that demons are not on my radar most days. I don't fret about evil spiritual beings. I have enough trouble with my own tendencies to sin and the sinfulness of the people who live around me. I said: "Why worry about demons when we're struggling with ourselves and others over forgiveness, anger, bitterness, lust, dishonesty, gossip, disrespect, greed? Those are the things that bring bondage and brokenness, right? Do we have to worry about forces of darkness, too?" Then I walked my listeners through the story to help them discover its main idea: *The good news of the kingdom is worth proclaiming and believing because Jesus has complete power and authority over the forces of darkness.*

At this point, I raised some questions: So what does this mean for our lives today? Do we struggle with the forces of darkness? If so, how does Jesus help us overcome them? These questions set up a brief sketch of a theology of spiritual warfare. In this sketch I argued that followers of Christ overcome the evil spiritual forces that battle us by resisting them with the resources provided by the gospel—not through magic or power encounters. I told my listeners that three key ideas emerge when we look at the entire sweep of Scripture. Here is the outline for this section of my sermon.

A. Our struggle with evil comes, in part, from evil spiritual forces.
   1. We face the world, the flesh, and the Devil (Eph. 2:1–3).

2. False teaching comes from demons (1 Tim. 4:1).

3. There are demons behind human conflicts (Eph. 6:12).

B. This struggle is more subtle in the West than in some places in the world (Eph. 6:12).

1. In Haiti, the sense of the demonic is more palpable because of voodoo.

2. In the United States, Satan's primary strategy is materialism or secularism even though there are demonic elements in popular culture.

C. Third, our approach is to use the resources provided by the gospel (Eph. 6:13–18).

1. We resist the Evil One by preaching the gospel to ourselves/others and by using or standing in the resources it provides (avoid occult—demon movies, video games).

2. There is no indication that exorcism or praying against territorial spirits is the way to operate.

This sketch took about ten minutes. My reason for sharing it is to provide an example of how a preacher can work elements of a biblical theology of spiritual warfare into a sermon. I closed the sermon with these words:

It was quite a day in the life of Jesus. The more I read Luke 4:31–44, the more I love it. There is nothing, absolutely nothing, that is more powerful or has more authority than Christ! Colossians 2:15 completes the picture: "And having disarmed the powers and authorities, he made a public spectacle of them, triumphing over them by the cross."

Be aware of evil spiritual forces. But don't fear! The apostle John wrote: "The one who is in you is greater than the one who is in the world" (1 John 4:4). Who is he talking about? Perhaps the Spirit who indwells us. But likely Jesus Christ in you, the hope of glory. After all, Christ dwells in us through his Spirit, the Spirit of Christ. Luke 4:31–44 says, greater is he who is among you than the forces of darkness that are in the world. That's why the good news of the kingdom is worth proclaiming!

At the risk of oversimplification, there are three main approaches to spiritual warfare by those who take it seriously.[6] During the 1990s, proponents of these views produced a spate of popular-level literature articulating their views and critiquing the other approaches. In my view, the best all-around treatment for pastors looking to develop or shore up their theology of spiritual warfare is *Three Crucial Questions about Spiritual Warfare* by Clinton E. Arnold.

Briefly, here are the three major views. At one end of the spectrum, the power-encounter approach calls for a direct approach to dealing with demonic forces, even to the point of identifying, praying against, binding, and evicting territorial spirits. Leading proponents include C. Peter Wagner, editor of *Breaking Strongholds* (1993), and Charles H. Kraft, author of *Defeating Dark Angels* (1992).

The view at the other end of the spectrum has been dubbed the gospel-encounter approach. It encourages believers to engage in spiritual warfare through repentance, faith, and obedience. It looks to Ephesians 6:10–20 as the key text for the strategy and resources that believers use. Leading proponents who have articulated this approach include John MacArthur,

How to Meet the Enemy (1992), and David Powlison, *Power Encounters: Reclaiming Spiritual Warfare* (1995).

A third approach, called the truth-encounter approach, differs significantly from the power-encounter approach. It is almost identical to the gospel-encounter approach except that truth-encounter proponents argue that believers can be "demonized" (see below). Leading truth-encounter proponents include Clinton E. Arnold, author of *Three Crucial Questions about Spiritual Warfare*, and Timothy M. Warner, *Spiritual Warfare: Victory over the Powers of This Dark World*. My theology of spiritual warfare aligns most closely with the truth-encounter approach.

Distinguish between the Descriptive and Prescriptive Aspects of Jesus' Encounter with Satan and His Demonic Forces

Perhaps the most challenging issue when preaching texts in which Jesus battles Satan and evil forces is to distinguish between what is descriptive and prescriptive. Are the actions and responses of Jesus in a particular pericope unique to his role as Messiah and Son of God? Are these actions or responses unique to the particular circumstances? Or do his actions and responses provide examples for his followers when they encounter the Evil One?

Followers of Jesus have no warrant to duplicate acts of Jesus that clearly flow from his power as the Messiah and Son of God. For example, Scripture gives us no hint that we are to command the winds and water and expect them to obey us as they obeyed Jesus (Luke 8:22–25). Only God has this power, and he does not appear to delegate it to human beings (see Ps. 107:23–31). Yet Scripture cites some clear actions of Jesus as examples to follow—particularly putting the interests of others ahead of our own and enduring suffering for doing good (Phil. 2:3–11; 1 Pet. 2:20–21). So how do we understand Jesus' sending out of the Twelve, giving them "power and authority to drive out all demons" (Luke 9:1)? Does this function as a mandate to all followers of Jesus at all times?

I asked three biblical scholars who do a fair share of preaching in the Gospels to weigh in on what criteria preachers should use in distinguishing between the descriptive and prescriptive aspects of Jesus' encounter with Satan and his demonic forces. These discussions resulted in the following insights that have helped me as I have preached the various gospel texts in which Jesus faces a showdown with the Evil One and the forces of darkness.

1. Begin with the Christological before moving to the exemplary.

Pastors often preach the story of Jesus' temptation in Matthew 4:1–11 and Luke 4:1–13 as a model for believers to use when they are tempted. Without denying the legitimacy of this practice, Grant Osborne wants us to begin with Christology. Osborne is a renowned New Testament scholar who preaches frequently and has spent a considerable amount of time over the years studying the Gospels. His most recent commentary on Matthew testifies to this.[7]

In his comments on Matthew 4:1–11, Osborne reminds us that this testing of Jesus is "the final event that launches Jesus' messianic ministry." By passing this test, Jesus "proves himself to be truly the Son of God, thus entering his ministry on a note of triumph."[8] Osborne concludes: "There is no hint in the context that Matthew is thinking of believers; it is Christological from start to finish."[9] What preachers need to communicate, then, is that Jesus is worth following and trusting because he is trustworthy. He is able to overcome the temptations of Satan. Whatever example a preacher might find in Jesus must be secondary to the Christological focus of the account.

2. When moving to the exemplary, look for patterns or common elements versus elements that occur only once.

After starting with the Christological, though, it is legitimate to look to Jesus as an example even as Paul did in Philippians 2:3–11 and Peter did in 1 Peter 2:20–21. But how does a preacher determine which aspects or details believers should replicate and which details are unique to the particular situation? My discussion with Gerry Breshears provided a way forward. Breshears serves as professor of systematic theology at Western Seminary in Portland, Oregon, where he teaches a course on Equipping for Spiritual Warfare. He is a member of the preaching team in his home church—Grace Community Church in Gresham, Oregon. When I asked him how preachers can decide whether to instruct listeners to emulate a particular practice of Jesus, he referred me to a general discussion of hermeneutical principles in *Vintage Church*, the book he coauthored with Mark Driscoll. These principles can help preachers navigate both what the Bible prescribes and describes. Breshears summarized the key points like this:

1. What the Bible prescribes, we do. We do what it commands us to be and do, and we do not do what it tells us not to do.
2. What the Bible describes, we follow as closely as possible. We look for principles in what the Bible describes and use these to guide our decisions (Acts 15:15–21; 1 Cor. 10:6–11).

3. Where the Bible is silent, God did not forget to say
   something. He was intentionally silent to allow for
   differences in our circumstances or culture so we
   can follow wisdom and the Spirit within the limits of
   prescription.[10]

In our conversation, Breshears brought up Matthew 4:1–11. Without denying the Christological emphasis of the text, he noted that the way Jesus used Scripture aligns with the pattern we see throughout Scripture. In fact, Jesus' first quotation from Deuteronomy 8:3 establishes the pattern: "Man shall not live on bread alone, but on every word that comes from the mouth of God" (Matt. 4:4). Psalm 119:11 reinforces this pattern when it says: "I have hidden your word in my heart that I may not sin against you." Not surprisingly, we find this pattern in Ephesians 6:10–20, perhaps the classic biblical text on spiritual warfare. There the resources that believers have at their disposal for engaging in spiritual warfare include both the "truth" (v. 14) and "the word of God" (v. 17).

Breshears made a final point that, he contends, a lot of believers ignore when they read the Gospels. He asked: "Is Jesus an example for us? Yes, he is living his life as a perfect, Spirit-controlled human being. He is not living his life as God."[11] Breshears, of course, affirms that Jesus is the God-man, the one who is fully God and fully human. But he wants us to remember that when Jesus became incarnate, he "did not consider equality with God something to be used to his own advantage" (Phil. 2:5). Rather, Jesus refrained from the independent use of his power as God. What we see in the Gospels is that Jesus accessed these only when the Spirit led him to do so. Significantly, both Matthew and Luke emphasize the role of the Spirit in Jesus' life at the outset of his temptation accounts (Matt. 4:1; Luke 4:1). So when we find patterns in Jesus' encounter with Satan and his evil forces, and when we find these patterns elsewhere in Scripture, we can legitimately preach them as examples.

3. Recognize that Jesus gave the authority to cast out demons to a rather wide circle of followers.

Now we turn to the more challenging task of preaching the exorcism texts. In the gospel accounts, Jesus frequently casts out or exorcises demons from human beings. He also "prescribes" exorcism as a work for his followers to do (Matt. 10:5–8; Mark 3:14–15; 6:7–13; Luke 9:1, 49–50; 10:17). But is this limited to the Twelve? Or is it a prescription that applies to all new covenant believers?

For help with this question, I turned to Craig Blomberg, distinguished professor of New Testament at Denver Seminary. While Blomberg is certainly "distinguished," he is an approachable guy who does a lot of preaching and personal ministry with all kinds of people, particularly the "left out and the right brained" at Scum of the Earth Church in downtown Denver, Colorado. He is a noted New Testament scholar whose writings include a commentary on the Gospel of Matthew and a work on interpreting the Bible coauthored with two of his colleagues.[12] In our conversation, Blomberg pointed out that while Jesus gave the Twelve power and authority to drive out demons, "It is not just the Twelve who have such powers. In the Gospels, the seventy-two receive the same power. So I would argue that any disciple can potentially exorcise demons."[13] Blomberg adds an important qualification, though: "Whereas Jesus cast out demons directly, his followers must do so in Jesus' name as so many other things in the early church were done—with Jesus' name standing for power or authority."[14]

But how closely do we follow the approach Jesus used to cast out demons? Again we turn to the second insight and distinguish between patterns or common elements and those elements that occur only once. Craig Blomberg made this observation. So did Gerry Breshears. In one of our conversations, Breshears pointed me to Mark 5:1–20, the account of Jesus restoring the demonized man in the region of the Gerasenes. Since Jesus asked for the demon's name in Mark 5:9–10, some emphasize the need for believers to do the same when they encounter demonized people. However, Breshears says: "Why is this the only time Jesus did this in the Gospels? We should look for what is common to all of the accounts. If an action is there only once, it is possible, but it is not required. We do not see any mention in the Epistles, particularly in Ephesians 6:10–20, about the need to know a demon's name."[15]

Now the fact that Jesus gave authority to cast out demons to a rather wide circle of followers does not mean that exorcism will be a primary or even a common means of engaging in spiritual warfare when we work with people who have succumbed to the world, the flesh, and the Devil. A close reading of the entire New Testament will not sustain this, so we do not want to give this impression in our preaching. But neither should we give the impression that exorcism is tied only to Jesus' earthly ministry.

Another key issue lurks behind the exorcism accounts in the Gospels, related to what is commonly called demon possession. The next insight speaks directly to this issue.

4. Point out the language used by the gospel writers when they speak of people being "demonized."

Clinton Arnold suggests that the Greek term *daimonizomai* is best rendered as "demonized" or "tormented by a demon" instead of "demon possessed."[16] He suggests this, noting that words for ownership or possession are absent in the Greek text.[17] The idea of possession likely slipped into our English translations due to Latin translations that used "the term *possessio* to describe a person deeply troubled by a demonic spirit."[18] The problem is that the derivative English term, *possession*, carries with it the idea of ownership or control. While this may be the case with a nonbeliever, Scripture is clear that "the issue of ownership is settled once and for all when a person turns to Christ."[19]

This leads to the question, whether a believer can be demon possessed. It is this issue that separates the gospel-encounter proponents from the truth-encounter proponents. For example, while Arnold affirms that a Christian cannot be owned or controlled by a demon, he asks if Christians can come under a high degree of influence by a demonic spirit: "Is it possible for Christians to yield control of their bodies to a demonic spirit in the same way that they yield to the power of sin?"[20] Though the believer's body is a temple of the Holy Spirit (1 Cor. 6:19), it does not follow that a demon cannot occupy the same space as the Spirit of God.[21] If evil can "reign" in a Christian's body (Rom. 6:12–13), if believers can give the Devil a "foothold" (Eph. 4:27), and if God's people under the old covenant could allow the temple to be the dwelling place for other gods and goddesses, is it not possible that demons can invade a believer and wield significant control when given the opportunity by the believer?[22]

Preachers will have to develop a theology of spiritual warfare and arrive at their own convictions about the degree of influence a demon can have over a believer. But preachers may help the discussion when they point out that "demonized" or "tormented by a demon" may capture the idea of the gospel writers better than "demon possessed."

For preachers who need to defend the idea of demons and demonization to listeners with a more naturalistic worldview, Grant Osborne suggests using the criterion of plausibility that is often employed in "historical Jesus" studies.[23] Essentially, this criterion looks for the most plausible scenario that accounts for the most data with the least amount of problems. In the case of a man who lives unclothed, resides in the tombs, shouts out Jesus' identity when he encounters him, and is able to break the chains that bind his hands and feet (Luke 8:26–29), demonization is more plausible than insanity. While insanity can account for some of the details, it cannot account for superhuman strength.

Abstract up from Cases of Demonization in the Gospels to Various Forms of Evil That Bring Bondage

A third strategy for preaching the "spiritual warfare texts" in the Gospels is to move up the "ladder of abstraction" from demonization to other forms of evil that bring bondage. Haddon Robinson uses the ladder of abstraction image to describe a preacher's movement up from the biblical world to cross over and move down to the modern setting.[24] Picture the left rail of the ladder as the biblical world and the right rail as the modern setting. Picture the rungs as moving from specific at the bottom to general at the top. Before moving from the left rail of the biblical world to the right rail of the modern setting, a preacher may need to move up the rungs of the ladder from a specific situation like demonization to a more general principle.

For example, moving upward from the rung of Jesus having the authority and power to cast out demons from people brings one to the more general rung of Jesus having control over evil forces. Once the preacher moves up to a more general rung and then uses it to move over to the right rail of the modern setting, the next step is to move back down the rungs to something more specific. So if we can trust Jesus as one who can cast out demons and thus as one who can control evil forces in general, we can trust Jesus to help us resist temptation to sin or to withstand persecution or to stand against the false teaching and false guilt that comes from Satan and his demons.

Grant Osborne says he preaches the gospel accounts about Jesus and his followers casting out demons in terms of spiritual warfare at a more general level.[25] He wants his listeners to understand that Satan is active today just as he was in the days of Jesus' earthly ministry. At the same time, he wants his listeners to understand that Satan is a defeated, bound foe (Matt. 12:29).

The basis for moving up and down the ladder of abstraction is the conviction that Scripture does not call believers to identify whether they are battling the world, the flesh, the Devil, or some combination of these forms of evil influence. Rather, we use the various weapons in Ephesians 6:10–20 to resist and overcome the Evil One.

Emphasize the "Already, but Not Yet" of the Kingdom when It Comes to Satan's Defeat

A final strategy for preaching gospel texts on Jesus' encounter with Satan and his forces is to emphasize the overlap in ages—the fact that the kingdom of God and Satan's defeat have arrived "already, but not yet." Preachers need to help their listeners realize that "we live at a time when the present evil age overlaps the age to come."[26] With the arrival of the kingdom and the sacrificial death of King Jesus, Satan and his forces are defeated enemies. That is the "already" aspect of the kingdom. The arrival of the kingdom was signaled in part by Jesus' acts of driving out demons (Matt. 12:28; Luke 11:20). But there is a "not yet" dimension. While Satan and his forces are defeated foes, they still carry on war in the world, blinding the minds of unbelievers (2 Cor. 4:4) and trying to devour believers (1 Pet. 5:8). It is an overstatement to say that Satan is alive and well on planet Earth.[27] But at least we can say that Satan, though a defeated enemy, is quite active on planet Earth. He is active now and until he is finally put in his place by God.

Emphasizing the "already, but not yet" aspect of Satan's demise will encourage listeners to be vigilant but not intimidated. We see Jesus modeling and teaching both a vigilance (to avoid sin) and a confidence (to avoid fear) in his encounter with Satan and his demonic forces. Our preaching must not do any less.

Whenever we preach, we may have listeners at one of two extremes. Darrell Bock, a noted gospels scholar, makes these observations:

> Some people see a demon behind every bush, while our culture, being enlightened, often makes the opposite error of dismissing such talk as reflecting a primitive worldview. Both approaches are a victory for the dark side. One never fights against what one does not believe is there. On the other hand, to be preoccupied with the demonic can produce a type of fixation that does not reflect spiritual balance and can deflect taking spiritual accountability.[28]

Faithful preachers serve Christ well when they do not skip the difficult gospel texts in which Jesus encounters Satan and the forces of darkness. Instead, faithful preachers take great effort to understand these texts truly and communicate them carefully. Our listeners need to hear the stories and teachings of Jesus that cry out that "the one who is in you is greater than the one who is in the world" (1 John 4:4).

6

ON PURPOSE

Aligning your application with the gospel writer's intent

Christian author John Eldredge recently discovered that a notorious drug cartel required its members to read his book *Wild at Heart.* He wrote this book to help men regain their masculinity and become the warriors and adventurers God wired them to be. Eldredge argues that this quest flows out of submission to Christ. But La Familia, a gang of cold-blooded killers founded in Michoacan, Mexico, has used the book to train its members and recruits—young men who will slay and behead anyone who hinders the gang's *cannabis* growing enterprise. Eldredge, of course, expressed outrage over this. He released a statement, saying: "It brings me sorrow and anger to know they are doing this, and I renounce their use of my words in this way."[1]

The last part of Eldredge's statement is haunting. "I renounce their use of my words in this way." I shudder a bit as I think about sermons I have preached from the Synoptic Gospels and the Gospel of John. Is it possible that Matthew, Mark, Luke, or John might say the same about the way I preach a text from one of their Gospels? Even worse, how might Jesus himself respond to the sermon I recently preached on the instructions he gives in Luke 10:1–24 to the seventy-two he sent out on a ministry campaign? Would Jesus say, "I renounce your use of my words in this way?"

To guard against this, we preachers work hard at our exegesis. We pore over the Greek text of the gospel pericope we intend to preach. We compare parallel accounts by studying a synopsis. We read up on Second Temple Judaism. We interact with the best commentaries. But oddly enough, the problem usually lies elsewhere than our exegesis. Haddon Robinson claims: "More heresy is preached in application than in Bible exegesis."[2] Yes, our application of the text is often the culprit. While heresy can crop up in the application of texts in any literary genre of Scripture, the danger is especially prevalent in the Gospels, given their unique mix of narrative and discourse.

One solution is to dispense with application altogether. But this will not do. David Jackman rightly argues:

> Every expositor knows that once the meaning of the biblical text has been stated and explained, its application to the contemporary hearers still remains to be spelled out. . . . While we know we cannot ourselves root God's Word into anyone's life, we should surely expect the Holy Spirit graciously to do this as we apply the Word to our current situations.[3]

Yet application often eludes even the most diligent preachers. Daniel Doriani, a New Testament scholar and pastor, confesses: "In my first fifteen years of preaching, I had methods for interpreting the Bible, but none for applying it."[4]

As soon as we commit ourselves to faithful application of texts in the four Gospels, we face a challenging question: to what extent are the descriptions of Jesus' deeds and words prescriptive for people today? For example, how do we apply Jesus' instructions not to take a purse or bag or footwear and not to greet anyone on the road when we set out to do missionary work (see Luke 10:4)? May I tell my listeners, based on Mark 4:35–41, that Jesus will always take them safely through the storms of life? I might apply Matthew 14:25–32 by saying to my listeners, "If you want to walk on water, you've got to get out of the boat."[5] But is this a faithful application?

In this chapter, I will propose a basic approach to application that attempts to align application with the author's intent. Then I will wrestle with how to apply a handful of texts from the Gospels to contemporary listeners by using the approach I have proposed.

An Approach to Applying Gospel Texts

A couple of decades ago, when my father and I both lived in Montana, we eagerly awaited September, the month when the green hue of leaves turns to yellow and red, and the morning air bites with cold and frost. We would pick up our bows and arrows, don our camouflage clothes, and head for the high mountain parks in hopes of getting a shot at an elk. We hunted in the Beartooth-Absaroka Wilderness Area, so I was always thankful for those who had blazed the trails ahead of us. One of our favorite spots was a thin strip of timber in a damp marsh wedged in between two peaks. We liked it because the elk liked it. Thankfully, a prospector decades before us had created a trail we could follow. We know he was responsible for the trail because the remains of his prospector's cabin still stand a few yards from the trail.

When it comes to applying the text of Scripture, particularly the Gospels, I am indebted to a couple of trailblazers whose tracks I follow closely as I work my way through the textual forest in pursuit of an application that seems as elusive as a six-point bull elk. The first is Craig Blomberg, a fine gospels scholar, and his coauthors, William Klein and Robert Hubbard, Jr. Their textbook, *Introduction to Biblical Interpretation*, contains a fine chapter on application that offers a four-step methodology.[6] A second scholar is Daniel M. Doriani, a former seminary professor of New Testament whose love for preaching and shepherding has taken him back to full-time pastoral ministry. Doriani has written a full-length treatment on the subject titled *Putting the Truth to Work: The Theory and Practice of Biblical Application*. I appreciate the work these scholars have done because of their rigorous exegesis of the text and their insistence that it must be applied to their own lives and the lives of God's people. After reflecting deeply on the methodology they propose, I have developed my own four-step approach.

1. Determine the text's original intent and application.

I concur with Doriani when he writes: "Linguistically, I believe authors can achieve their goals. Therefore, I speak of authorial intent, knowing that critics of authorial intent still expect their readers to seek their intended meaning."[7] It is almost universally accepted that the biblical writers wrote not simply to explain a subject but to achieve an object. They wrote to instruct God's people, to challenge the way they lived, to shape their thoughts and behaviors (see 2 Tim. 3:16–17). So authorial intent extends to application.

Before examining exactly how Matthew, Mark, Luke, and John intended for us to read their Gospels, we will do well to note the seven ways that the Bible instructs us. Doriani explains: "The Bible is not a set of instructions, but all of it is instructive.

Every text is meaningful. Biblical texts instruct us seven ways: through rules, ideals, doctrines, redemptive acts in narratives, exemplary acts in narratives, biblical images, and songs and prayers."[8] I would argue that the Gospels instruct their audiences through a combination of all of these ways. But specifically, what are the gospel writers trying to accomplish through their Gospels?

In 2002, after several decades of extensive research on the function of Old Testament narrative literature, I argued that the biblical authors were writing to communicate theology and not simply to record history.[9] Now, after similar research on the Gospels and two-and-a-half decades of preaching them, I conclude that the Gospels work in similar fashion. They are historical and biographical, but they are more than historical and biographical accounts. The Gospels are accounts that proclaim the person and work of Jesus Christ as good news. Klein, Blomberg, and Hubbard call the Gospels "theological biographies."[10] Sidney Greidanus notes that "the goal of their composition is preaching, kerygma."[11]

This perspective gets obscured by the view that direct teaching has priority over narrative. This view has been popularized by an otherwise outstanding treatment of biblical literary forms—and one of my personal favorites on the topic—by Gordon Fee and Douglas Stuart. In their book *How to Read the Bible for All Its Worth*, Fee and Stuart state: "Narratives are precious to us because they so vividly demonstrate God's involvement in the world and illustrate his principles and calling. They thus teach us a lot—but what they directly teach us does not systematically include personal ethics. For this area of life, we must turn elsewhere in the Scriptures—to the various places where personal ethics are actually taught categorically and explicitly."[12]

However, Craig Blomberg cites 2 Timothy 3:16 and argues that "narrative is as much a database for theology as any other genre."[13] Doriani questions Fee and Stuart's view, asking "how one can argue that narrative is normative only if backed by explicit teaching" when "(1) the principle is itself extrabiblical and (2) Scripture is fundamentally a narrative account of God's redemption. The speeches of Moses, the declamations of the prophets, the letters of the apostles are not freestanding. They frequently comment upon or draw conclusions from narrative. When they do, the narrative is foundational and the ethic is derivative."[14]

Doriani also argues that "though we must critique moralistic uses of Scripture, Scripture does offer moral guidance in narrative."[15] To be sure, "Biblical narrative dwells on redemption before ethics, yet narratives do invite readers to identify with characters and find spiritual direction or warning."[16] According to Doriani, "Jesus himself justifies the search for ethical principles from biblical narratives" based on his use of Scripture in response to Satan's temptation (Matt. 4:4, 7) and his response to the Pharisees when they questioned his Sabbath observance (Matt. 12:1–7).[17]

As already noted, the Gospels constitute a specific kind of narrative. They function as theological biographies that proclaim the person and work of Jesus the Messiah as good news. As such, they communicate theology to the Christian communities. Each gospel writer has unique theological concerns he addresses as he writes to a particular community. Preachers must pay careful attention to these emphases. For example, I recently preached a Palm Sunday sermon on Luke's account of Jesus' so-called triumphal entry in Luke 19:28–44. I was struck with how Luke emphasized the fact that Jesus' reign brings peace to those who accept him as king. Luke leaves out details that the other Synoptic Gospels include. He says nothing about people spreading branches on the road and shouting, "Hosanna!" But he includes a cry of praise from the crowd that Matthew and Mark do not: "Peace in heaven and glory in the highest!" (v. 38). This cry is reminiscent of the angels' praise before the shepherds at Jesus' birth: "Glory to God in the highest heaven, and on earth peace to those on whom his favor rests" (Luke 2:14). Lest we wonder how much to make of the crowd's cry of peace when Jesus enters Jerusalem, the very next pericope records Jesus' lament: "If you, even you, had only known on this day what would bring you peace—but now it is hidden from your eyes" (Luke 19:41).

Once we have correctly determined a text's original intent and application, we are ready to take a second step in the process of faithfully applying the text to the lives of our listeners.

2. Determine the underlying principle that is transferable to today's listeners.

This second step is common to all literary genres of Scripture and to both Testaments. The various instructions—whether they come in the form of rules, ideals, doctrines, redemptive acts in narratives, exemplary acts in narratives, biblical images, or songs and prayers—may or may not be immediately transferable. Wise interpreters and preachers need to discover whether or not the principle or theological message is right on the surface or lies a layer or two beneath it. There are two considerations here: culture and salvation history.

To begin with, we must ask if the cultural conditions identified in a Gospel or assumed by its authors limit its application in its present form to a particular culture in a particular time.[18] To put this another way, we must ask if "the particular cultural form expressed in the biblical text [is] present today, and if so does it have the same significance as it did then?"[19]

For example, in Luke 5:17–26, Jesus heals a paralytic whose friends were so determined to get him to Jesus that they lowered him through the roof of a house when the crowd around Jesus hindered their access. Jesus commends their faith, forgives the man's sin, and heals him so that he can walk. The principle on the surface is that Jesus commends the faith of those who lower their friends through rooftops of houses where Jesus is preaching when they are unable to get through a crowd. It does not take a gospels scholar to see immediately that the cultural conditions today do not allow the principle to be transferred as it is. The construction of modern houses differs greatly from the simple four-room houses common in first-century Palestine. Cutting through the roof of a house in Galilee in the time of Jesus was not an easy chore—the roofs were made of reeds and branches covered with plaster and placed on wooden beams— but it was at least possible.[20] Today, by the time you removed the asphalt shingles and cut through the wood sheeting covering the trusses, you would still have to drop down through attic space and then through insulation to reach the Sheetrock ceiling of the room below it. So it is highly unlikely, given the building practices in our current culture, that the kind of faith Jesus commends will involve cutting through the roof of a house.

There is an underlying principle in this account, though, which can be transferred. The underlying principle is that people with faith will fight through whatever obstacles keep them from getting their friends and themselves to Christ. Doriani wisely observes:

> When believers talk about seeking God's will, we often say, "We will wait and see if God will open a door or close a door."

Perhaps. But this story suggests that sometimes the door is open, sometimes the door is closed, and sometimes we have to tear the door off its hinges, whether by ourselves or with the help of friends. The Bible's quest stories teach us that true faith fights through obstacles and temporary defeats.[21]

The other matter that determines the nature of transferability is a gospel text's setting in the flow of salvation history. The events of the Gospels occur in an era of transition from the old covenant associated with Moses to the new covenant inaugurated through Christ. Also, the kingdom of God has been inaugurated but awaits complete fulfillment. On the one hand, Jesus proclaims that the kingdom of God has come near (Mark 1:15) and that his ability to drive out demons is proof that the kingdom of God has come upon people (Matt. 12:28). On the other hand, Jesus teaches his followers to pray "your kingdom come" (Matt. 6:10) and speaks of the kingdom of God arriving in the future (Matt. 25:1–13, 31–44). So we can say that the kingdom of God has arrived "already, but not yet." What does this mean for our interpretation and application of the Gospels? Quite simply, we are dealing with a time in salvation history when there is an overlap of ages.[22] The future has been pulled back into the present. So when we make application of gospel texts to present-day listeners, we must keep in mind that some things Jesus taught do not transfer exactly into the new covenant age.

For example, what do we make of Jesus' repeated instructions to keep his identity and actions concealed? When Jesus healed a man with leprosy, Jesus instructed him not to tell anyone (Mark 1:43–44). Jesus also gave strict orders not to let anyone know about his raising of a twelve-year-old girl from death (Mark 5:43). Then, after Peter's declaration that Jesus is the Messiah, Jesus warned the disciples "not to tell anyone about him" (Mark 8:30). From this, we should not deduce a transferable principle that calls for us to conceal Jesus' identity. Instead, we realize that this approach was needed in a climate of Messianic misunderstanding. People were anticipating a Messiah who would overthrow the Romans—not one whose deliverance would come through the path of suffering and death. Revealing his identity too soon in his ministry would set in motion events —namely his arrest and crucifixion—that needed to wait for later. Today there is no reason to withhold either Jesus' identity or reports about his miraculous deeds.

Now we are ready to go back and explore the challenge of knowing whether the author's intent in a particular text is to call Jesus' followers to a certain action or to call them to belief in a particular aspect of Jesus' character. Even the latter may create a renewed confidence or trust in Jesus that leads to a particular action. So consider a third step.

3. Determine what exemplary elements we might follow in the imitation of Christ.

Protestant New Testament scholars have often been as wary of using Christ as an example as they have been about their Greek students using interlinear New Testaments. When it comes to the imitation of Christ, they are afraid of misusing the text and short-circuiting the interpretive process. They are afraid of a sentimental, less-than-thoughtful approach to the text that ignores the Evangelists' emphases and rushes straight to any examples that Jesus provides. There is also a concern that this approach leads to a works-oriented approach to Christian living that is at odds with the gospel.

Yet the imitation-of-Christ motif is embedded in Scripture and cannot be ignored. Once again, Doriani offers a helpful apologetic for preaching the words and works of Jesus as examples to imitate: "Jesus himself commanded his disciples to follow his example. They must be willing to work for the kingdom, as he was (Matt. 16:21–26; Mark 8:31–37; Luke 9:21–25). They must serve, just as he did not come to be served, but to serve (Matt. 20:28; Mark 10:45)."[23] Lest we think these are isolated cases, consider what Jesus said to his disciples as recorded in Luke 6:40: "The student is not above the teacher, but everyone who is fully trained will be like their teacher." Even the night before his crucifixion, Jesus called his disciples to follow his example and wash each other's feet (John 13:14–16).

Doriani reminds us, too, that the apostles who authored the New Testament Epistles continued this emphasis on imitating Jesus,

> explaining how and why believers are to imitate Christ. Conformity to Christ is our destiny (Rom. 8:29; 1 Cor. 15:49; 1 John 3:2–3); it is also our obligation. John said, if we claim to live in Christ, we must walk as Jesus walked (1 John 2:6) and lay down our lives for others as Jesus laid down his life for us.[24]

Paul insisted as strongly as John did on the imitation of Christ. He

> set Christ's life as the pattern for love and forgiveness in the church (Eph. 4:32; 5:2). We must prefer the interests of others over our own, as Jesus did (Phil. 2:3–8). Christ's love is also a paradigm for the family: husbands should love their wives as Christ loved the church, sacrificing himself for her (Eph. 5:25–27). Regarding himself as an example to his churches (Phil. 3:17; 2 Thess. 3:7), he urges people to imitate him as he imitates Christ (1 Cor. 4:16; 11:1; Phil. 4:9).[25]

The apostle Peter even used Christ's attitude in the atonement as a model of how Christians should endure suffering (1 Pet. 2:18–25), while the writer of Hebrews presented Jesus' experience of "suffering to glory" as the course that his followers can expect to follow (10:32–12:4).

But are there any limits? Can preachers challenge listeners to follow any and every example we find in the earthly life of Jesus? In addition to the general limits related to an example being culture bound or salvation-era bound, there are three limits uniquely related to the actions of Jesus himself.

First, some elements are so closely tied to events in Jesus' earthly life that few Bible teachers would say we should expect them to occur literally in our lives today, even if these elements could conceivably be duplicated in the way they occurred in the Bible. A case in point is Peter's attempt to walk on water as Jesus did, in Matthew 14:22–33. This is an isolated incident in the Gospels—unlike repeated calls by Jesus for his disciples to serve as he did (Mark 10:45; John 13:14–16).

At the same time, here is an example of an action in which we can find a principle for imitation. This is what John Ortberg gets at in his book *If You Want to Walk on Water, You've Got to Get Out of the Boat.* Ortberg recognizes that though our circumstances will be quite different, there are still situations that will produce fear in us and keep us from extreme discipleship—stepping out in faith to obey Jesus.[26] Grant Osborne handles the application of this text in a similar fashion. While he recognizes the Christology of the passage—that it "comes the closest in Matthew to establishing the deity of Christ"—he also sees it teaching that believers gain "victory through depending totally on Christ."[27] Osborne continues:

When Peter asked to walk on the water, that was the response Jesus wished. As long as Peter focused on Jesus, he was able to take step after step on the water. However, when he turned to consider the earthly situation, he failed and began to sink into the depths. The entire NT builds on this, as victory over sin and temptation is completely related to the degree to which we are centered wholly on Christ.[28]

I believe we see this kind of movement from a specific action of Jesus to a more general principle when Paul says to the Corinthian church: "We always carry around in our body the death of Jesus, so that the life of Jesus may also be revealed in our body" (2 Cor. 4:10). Jesus himself called his followers to experience crucifixion in a more generalized—as opposed to literal—way when he said: "Whoever wants to be my disciple must deny themselves and take up their cross daily and follow me" (Luke 9:23). To summarize, there are times when the inability to duplicate the exact experience Jesus had with his disciples here on earth will limit the way that a preacher calls for the imitation of Christ. In such a case, there will be either no application or an indirect application.

Second, the imitation of Christ may be limited or contradicted by the immediate or larger context of Scripture. Klein, Hubbard, and Blomberg want us to ask if the "larger context of the same book of Scripture in which the passage appears limit[s] the application in any way or . . . promote[s] a more universal application?" Furthermore, "does subsequent revelation limit the application of a particular passage even if the book in which it appears does not?" Finally, "is the specific teaching 'contradicted' elsewhere in ways that show it was limited to exceptional situations?"[29] A classic example is Jesus' instructions to the seventy-two in Luke 10:4: "Do not take a purse or bag or sandals; and do not greet anyone on the road." Yet later in Luke's Gospel, we hear Jesus telling his followers to go ahead and take a purse and bag and even a sword (Luke 22:36).[30] Jesus is clearly not contradicting himself, because he acknowledges that his earlier set of instructions were different, as well as effective (Luke 22:35)! The reason for the change seems to lie with the different ministry climate the disciples will face. Joel Green comments: "In times to come, the apostles can no longer depend on a warm welcome, but must prepare themselves for hostility, even of a violent sort."[31]

This limit is also helpful when interpreting a text like Jesus' conversation with the rich ruler in Luke 18:18–30. Are we to follow Jesus' example and tell every wealthy person with whom we share the gospel to sell all possessions and give to the poor? When I preached on this text recently, I noted that Zacchaeus was commended by Jesus three pericopes later for giving half of his possessions to the poor (Luke 19:8–9). There is, of course, a substantial difference between all and half! Furthermore, the account in Luke 19:1–10 shows a quite different approach. Jesus simply commands Zacchaeus to come and allow Jesus to stay at his house. There is no mention of giving possessions to the poor, even though Zacchaeus responds by doing so. The simplicity of Jesus' call to Zacchaeus is more aligned with the reception of the kingdom of God like a little child (see Luke 18:15–17). The lesson is clear: we must always pay attention to the context to make sure we do not turn what Jesus does or says into models to imitate in all situations at all times.

Finally, there is a third limitation upon the imitation of Christ. The imitation of Christ may be limited by actions that are clearly tied to Jesus' unique role as Son of God and Messiah.

When Jesus calms the storm in Mark 4:35–41 and the parallel synoptic accounts (Matt. 8:23–27; Luke 8:22–25), his disciples respond with fear and ask: "Who is this? Even the wind and the waves obey him!" (Mark 4:41). Such a question has its basis in their knowledge from Psalm 107:23–30 that calming storms at sea is something that only God does. The application will certainly have to do with faith, as Jesus suggests in Mark 4:40, and not with imitating Jesus' act of calming sea storms or other "storms" of life.

To be sure, Jesus does grant the Twelve the power to heal the sick and raise the dead (Matt. 10:8)—actions that point to his power as Israel's Messiah. In a case like this, we cannot prohibit application by placing it in the category of "things that only God and his Son can do." Rather, depending on your theology (cessasionist or continuationist), you may want to go back to the second limitation where we look at whether or not the surrounding context of Scripture places limits on our imitation of Christ. While Paul acknowledges that some believers have gifts of healing (1 Cor. 12:9), I question whether the broader context of the New Testament teaches that all believers should be able to heal the sick or that any aside from the apostles should be expected to raise the dead.

The time spent on developing these limitations should not dampen our enthusiasm for imitating Christ. Rather, it should free us to pursue the imitation of Christ within the bounds of Scripture and our theology. Doriani's counsel is worth pondering:

> Since the imitation motif suffuses the New Testament, every narrative of Jesus' actions becomes relevant. When training select groups, we note that Jesus chose a core group of

twelve. We befriend agnostics, deists, and polytheists because Jesus befriended sinners. We say, "Writing a check is not enough," and stress involvement in mercy ministries because Jesus touched the unclean. We do not require an independent imperative to verify these points. Jesus' life is enough.[32]

We have now surveyed three steps for applying the teaching of the gospel texts to our lives and the lives of our listeners. These three steps lead us to a fourth and decisive step.

4. Make application that aligns with the text's original intent and application.

In the previous steps, we considered the options for application. Now it is time to make specific applications for ourselves and our listeners. The operative word here is *specific*. In my experience, vague application leads to vague Christian living. The challenge is to act specifically and decisively on what we read in the Gospels and then call our listeners to respond similarly to what we preach from the gospel accounts.

The starting point should always be the author's intent. We must prayerfully consider whether the author's intended application to his original audience is exactly what our listeners need to believe or do. If so, our task will be relatively simple. But we live in a different historical-cultural setting. We face the same challenges and pressures, but they come to us in different forms. The disciples of Jesus undoubtedly struggled with lust and greed and anger. But the disciples did not struggle with Internet porn. Nor did they rack up credit card debt. Nor did they have to apologize for what they tweeted or texted on their smart phones. Life works differently today. So sometimes we may need to dig deeper for an underlying principle that is applicable to our listeners. Of course we must always be alert for the ways Jesus lived, loved, served, and worshiped. These will become examples to imitate.

If our application takes a slightly different direction than the Evangelist's application, we will do well to ask if it still aligns with his intent. Over the years, I have asked myself a question when I wrestle with the application of biblical texts, including those from the four Gospels. Could the author of this text envision my application given the different historical-cultural context in which I am preaching? To put it another way, given the unique challenges my people are facing, and given the prevalent worldviews in the culture in which they live, would Matthew, Mark, Luke, or John be all right with the application I make from a particular account they wrote? As Jack Kuhatschek says, "If an application does not arise out of the divine and human authors' intent, then it does not carry the authority of God's Word, even though it may be helpful and insightful."[33]

To help put theory into practice, I want to turn now to a handful of texts from the Gospels and wrestle with how we might apply them to ourselves and our listeners. You will benefit from reading each text slowly and thoughtfully before reading my thoughts on how to apply it.

Luke 17:11–19

The story of Jesus healing the ten lepers is a challenge to apply because, at first glance, "its relevance seems slight."[34] The fact that it contains the various themes of miracle stories makes it a candidate, says Doriani, for a boring exposition.[35] Yes, the themes are familiar: Jesus is compassionate, Jesus restores things, Jesus is Lord, miracles summon faith, and miracles accomplish salvation. But there is no moral imperative in this narrative—at least not an explicit one. The only imperative Jesus offers to the Samaritan leper who returned with praise and thanksgiving is "Rise and go" (Luke 17:19). So what is a preacher to do with this text?

The key is recognizing what the account says about faith. Faith is a key theme in this part of Luke's so-called "travel narrative," as Jesus teaches his followers what it means to walk with God while he is traveling to Jerusalem. Faith is prominent in the previous account (17:5–6), and it appears again two pericopes later in the parable of the persistent widow (18:1–8). Then, while the term *faith* does not appear in the parable of the two men who went up to the temple to pray (18:9–14) and the account of the rich ruler (18:18–30), genuine faith is clearly being described. At the end of the chapter, though, the account of the blind beggar contains Jesus' pronouncement that the blind man's faith has saved him (18:34–43). I agree with Doriani when he says that Luke 17:11–19 "sheds light on saving faith."[36] In this account, Jesus shows common grace to ten lepers who were helpless and homeless (vv. 11–14). The lone leper to return teaches us that those who turn to Jesus in faith receive the Lord's saving grace (vv. 15–19). In this final section, it is quite clear that the evidence of saving faith is gratitude. The leper who returned—ironically a Samaritan!—"threw himself at Jesus' feet and thanked him" (v. 16).

As I neared the end of my sermon, I made the observation that those who are not grateful to God for his common grace either miss out on his saving grace or at least end up taking it for granted. Then I made application by calling my listeners to cultivate gratitude. I was careful to frame this in terms of the gospel of Christ. I emphasized that gratitude is a gospel virtue—that is, something the gospel produces in us. Yet it is also a virtue we must cultivate. After all, Paul tells the Thessalonian church to "give thanks in all circumstances; for this is God's will for you in Christ Jesus" (1 Thess. 5:18). I even offered some specific suggestions as to how my listeners might do this. I encouraged them to build thanksgiving into all of their prayers, to give thanks before they eat their meals, to fall asleep counting their blessings, and to use communion as a time for giving thanks—something we recognize as inherent to communion whenever we call it the Eucharist (which is related to the Greek expression for giving thanks).

I did not find an example of Christ in this text to imitate. Nor did I have to go below the surface to find a principle beneath a teaching of Jesus that was either culture bound or salvation-era bound. Nor did I simply latch onto something the returning leper did and turn it into a moral imperative. Rather, I wrestled with the author's intent until I determined that he intended to explain what saving faith is by sharing this account. Then I figured out that the author wanted his listeners to understand that gratitude is the mark of saving faith. Once I figured this out, it was quite clear that I needed to cultivate gratitude in my own life and to encourage my listeners to do the same.

Luke 10:1–16

Let me return to a challenging text to which I referred earlier—Jesus' instructions to the seventy-two disciples in Luke 10:1–16. When I preached this text in a recent series on Luke's Gospel, I concluded that it serves to instruct Jesus' disciples on what they should expect and do as servants of Christ who are sent on a mission. Even though the instructions were given to the seventy-two, I see ample material in the Gospels and in the New Testament that all believers are sent on Christ's missions. I pointed out that Jesus modifies these instructions a bit in Luke

22:35–38 for serving in more hostile environments. But neither that discussion nor anything else in the New Testament suggests that these instructions were so uniquely attached to a particular time and place that they cannot be instructive for our contemporary situation. While I avoid "list preaching" unless I am in a passage that clearly has a list, it was quite obvious that Jesus does provide a list of insights about gospel ministry—both expectations and tasks for disciples. Here are the principles I identified along with some of the applications I suggested.

1. There is always a need for more workers (v. 2). Here I encouraged my listeners to pray for their children and grandchildren to be "ministers." I also challenged the listeners in my affluent context to use their retirement for ministry. I cited the example of my best friend's father, LaRue Goetz, who was that very week in Ukraine helping with a church planting effort even at seventy-seven years of age! I suggested that in our context, our retirees might spend time as volunteer staff members, jail ministry volunteers, community Bible study leaders, and children's ministry workers. I encouraged young parents to get their young children involved in serving.

2. Workers can expect resistance (vv. 3, 10). Here I reminded my listeners that not everyone would receive them well when they shared the gospel. I also said that going out as a lamb among wolves implied going with gentleness and not the bombast that some Christian workers employ.

3. Workers must not get distracted (v. 4b). I pointed out that, in light of Luke 22:36, the instruction not to take a purse or bag or sandals was not universal but likely

indicated the seventy-two were being sent on a short-term trip. Neither the carrying of extra items nor the time spent greeting people on the way were to be distractions. I told my listeners I would not attempt to list all the distractions they face when trying to do ministry, but I encouraged them to make their own list!

4. Workers bring a message of peace and judgment (vv. 5–6, 11–15). Here I pointed out that the words "peace to this house" are not a slogan but an offer of goodwill from God (see Isa. 52:7). I stressed that what we share is the gospel of the kingdom, that the kingdom of God has arrived in Jesus, and that those who reject God's peace will receive God's judgment. I noted the lengthy instructions Jesus gave about announcing judgment in verses 11–15 as a reminder that we must not shrink back from telling people about the consequences of rejecting the gospel.

5. Workers may earn wages from their work (v. 7). I mentioned how this shapes the way we look at a church budget that spends a lot of money on salaries for both staff and missionaries. There is no need to fret over the money we pay Christian workers. It is a tremendous investment. At the same time, I insisted that those who do not earn their wages from gospel ministry are no less significant than those who do. This, of course, is not a specific application Jesus makes. But given the situation of my listeners, who live in a community near a world-class evangelical seminary and worship next to leading Bible scholars and Christian educators, I felt I needed to make this point and that it aligned with what Jesus was saying.

6. God takes the response to his workers personally (v. 16). Finally, I wanted my listeners to understand that when they have faithfully proclaimed the message, they have spoken for God and that God will hold people accountable for how they respond.

Mark 4:35–41

A final text I want to consider is Mark 4:35–41. Over the years, I have heard quite a few sermons on this magnificent story of Jesus calming the storm. Invariably preachers will call listeners to trust Jesus when they face the storms of life, knowing that Jesus will get them through the storm. However, this account is a good example of a story that does not get interpreted and applied as precisely as it should unless the preacher has paid close attention to the context.

The key to understanding this story lies in the two parables that immediately precede it in Mark 4:26–32. Both of these parables emphasize that the kingdom of God will succeed even though we can't make it grow ourselves and even though it starts out so small. Read in light of these parables, the disciples' fear seems to stem from a concern for more than physical safety. These men had turned their backs on their careers and had broken family ties to follow Jesus. The panic that hit them in that boat was more than the fear of losing their lives. It was the fear that the cause for which they had given their lives was going to sink. They feared that Jesus would never be king over this great kingdom and that they had given their lives to a lost cause. Mark 4:35–41 affirms, though, that you can be certain that you have invested your life in a successful enterprise because the kingdom depends on a King who has unlimited power.

The application of this text, then, is not simply to trust Jesus to get you through the storms of life. It is to keep from losing heart, from fearing that you have given your life to a lost cause when you see the growth of Islam, the seeming ineffectiveness of your church, and a host of teens in your youth group who go off to college and walk away from the faith they were taught. Whenever we are tempted to give up or give out, we continue to serve Jesus because the kingdom of God depends on him, the King who has the power to see it established.

Doing What the Lord Says

Every April I travel to Bozeman with a close friend to fly-fish the Madison River in Montana. My friend Dave and I have a favorite stretch near the mouth of the Bear Trap Canyon that is thick with rainbow trout. Unfortunately, to get there, we have to walk through terrain that is thick with rattlesnakes. We have concluded that the reward outweighs the risk. I feel the same way about preaching the Gospels. Some preachers I know shy away from the Gospels, except for an occasional foray into the Sermon on the Mount (Matt. 5–7) or the Upper Room discourse (John 13–17) or the birth narratives of Jesus when Christ or Advent arrives. They fear the perils of trying to apply these texts to modern listeners.

Let me say that such fear is legitimate. It is what has prompted me to write this chapter. I do not want to say in the name of Christ what he or the gospel writers really did not intend to say. But those who neglect the Gospels have a much bigger fear. In Luke's version of Jesus' "Sermon on the Mount," he records Jesus as saying:

> Why do you call me, "Lord, Lord," and do not do what I say? As for everyone who comes to me and hears my words and

puts them into practice, I will show you what they are like. They are like a man building a house, who dug down deep and laid the foundation on rock. When a flood came, the torrent struck that house but could not shake it, because it was well built. But the one who hears my words and does not put them into practice is like a man who built a house on the ground without a foundation. The moment the torrent struck that house, it collapsed and its destruction was complete. (Luke 6:46–49)

What we should fear most is not sharing Jesus' words with his followers and helping them understand how to practice them. Their destiny hangs in the balance, and God has chosen to use us as his spokespeople to herald the words and works of his Son, Jesus the Messiah. So preach the Gospels with heart, soul, mind, and strength! Trust that the guidelines shared in this chapter will help you preach gospel texts with accuracy and faithfulness to their authors' intent. In more than a decade of fishing in the Bear Trap Canyon, my friend Dave and I have had one close call with a rattlesnake. But we have not been struck because we have proceeded with reasonable caution. Take the same approach to preaching the Gospels, and you will put your listeners in a position to build their lives on rock rather than sand.

7

AGAINST COUNTERFEITS

Affirming the authority of the four
Gospels over the lost gospels

It was a dark and stormy night. I was driving my family from our home near Bozeman, Montana, to Wenatchee, Washington, to spend Thanksgiving with relatives. During the drive I was mesmerized by the audiobook to which I was listening—*The Da Vinci Code* by Dan Brown. Like all good novels, its plot twists and plot turns kept me entertained. At the same time, the story line deeply disturbed me. My "disturbia" reached its climax when I got to the part where one of the characters, Sir Leigh Teabing, a British royal historian and an expert on the Holy Grail, begins talking about the Bible. "History has never had a definitive version of the book. . . . More than *eighty* gospels were considered for the New Testament, and yet only a relative few were chosen for inclusion—Matthew, Mark, Luke, and John among them."[1] Teabing's tirade continued with the claim that the church, motivated by its own political agenda and thirst for power, suppressed these other gospels. As a result, "almost everything our fathers taught us about Christ is *false*."[2]

Although Sir Leigh Teabing is a fictional scholar, at least two other real-life scholars put these "lost gospels" in the spotlight at the dawn of the twenty-first century. Both began their journeys as evangelicals. Both hold notable professorships at world-class universities. And while neither would sign off on some of the more laughable, sensational claims in Brown's novel, both have touted the lost gospels as a source for a Jesus more to their liking than the Jesus proclaimed by the Gospels of Matthew, Mark, Luke, and John. Their journeys are worth a brief look since some of the people to whom you have preached have followed them— whether directly in indirectly.

A Tale of Two Scholars

Elaine Pagels, professor of religion at Princeton, joined an evangelical church when she was fourteen and found herself fascinated with the Gospel of John.[3] When she entered college, she decided to learn Greek to read the New Testament in its original language, hoping to discover the source of its power. But when she entered the Ph.D. program at Harvard, she was astonished to learn from other students that her professors had file cabinets full of "gospels" and "apocrypha" written during the first centuries. These writings contained sayings and rituals attributed to Jesus. These materials had been discovered in 1945 among a cache of texts unearthed near Nag Hammadi in Upper Egypt. Pagels recalls: "When my fellow students and I investigated these sources, we found that they revealed diversity within the Christian movement that later, 'official' versions of Christian history had suppressed so effectively that only now, in the Harvard graduate school, did we hear about them."[4]

Pagels soon found herself challenged not only intellectually but also spiritually. One particular saying of Jesus in the *Gospel of Thomas* struck her as self-evidently true: "If you bring forth what is within you, what you bring forth will save you. If you do not bring forth what is within you, what you do not bring forth will destroy you."[5] Imagine that. Jesus is not telling his followers what to believe but challenges them to discover what lies hidden within themselves. Pagels adopted this as the mantra that guided her through the tragic twists of her own story—the loss of a young son to illness and the loss of her husband in a mountain-climbing accident. She cast her lot with a Jesus who "directs each disciple to discover the light within" rather than the Jesus who insists that he is the light of the world.[6]

Four-hundred-seventy miles to the south and west of Princeton, another professor enamored with the lost gospels holds a significant position at a respected university. Bart Ehrman is a professor of religious studies at the University of North Carolina, Chapel Hill. Like Pagels, Ehrman had a "born-again" experience in high school and set out to get the training he needed to become a "serious" Christian.[7] He entered the Moody Bible Institute in Chicago and became passionate in his quest for knowledge about the Bible. After graduate work at Wheaton College where he learned Greek, Ehrman headed for Princeton Theological Seminary to pursue doctoral studies under the revered scholar Bruce Metzger, a giant in the field of Greek biblical manuscripts. Ehrman, by his own account, came to Princeton "passionate, and armed to take on those liberals with their watered-down view of the Bible. As a good evangelical Christian I was ready to fend off any attacks on my biblical faith."[8] But things did not go as planned. What he learned led him to change his mind about the Bible. And in the process, he, like Pagels, became fond of the lost gospels and the great "diversity of early Christianities."[9]

What Is at Stake in Your Preaching

In one sense Pagels and Ehrman and the lost gospels are old news. It has been almost a decade since these two found themselves in the popular spotlight and since a spate of books and programs on the Discovery Channel or the History Channel dissected the controversy. But, as is so often the case, while the frenzy over the lost gospels has subsided, their impact has not. The conviction that the lost gospels are as authoritative and beneficial as the four Gospels is simply accepted as fact by the general populace—including some of the people who find their way into the worship services in which you preach.

This presents preachers with a challenge. While our task is to proclaim the four Gospels, there are times when we need to defend them against the views of skeptics and heretics. Like the author of Jude, our intent when we preach is to communicate the good news, "the salvation we share," but it is sometimes necessary to shift gears and "contend for the faith that was once for all entrusted to God's holy people" (Jude 3). In our day, contending for the faith requires defending the historical reliability and the supreme authority of the four Gospels, as well as the rest of Scripture. But how can we do this in our preaching of the Gospels? And who can we look to for guides? What scholars have followed similar educational paths as Pagels and Ehrman, studying at world-class evangelical and "secular" institutions under world-class scholars, and have not found it necessary to jettison their evangelical convictions?

A Tale of Two More Scholars

Meet Craig Blomberg, or if you have been reading the chapters in this volume sequentially, meet him again. According to

Blomberg himself, it is uncanny how similar his background is to Bart Ehrman's.[10] Both grew up in mainline Protestant churches in the Midwest. Both had a conversion experience in high school through a prominent evangelical campus ministry. Both graduated from high school in 1973. Both went on to small, private, church-related undergraduate colleges in Illinois. Both went to evangelical graduate schools in Chicagoland for masters' degrees. Both landed in an internationally known university with a prestigious divinity school for Ph.D. work, to pursue careers as New Testament scholars and professors. (I might add that from the looks of their promotional photos, both sport the same scruffy beards!)

But the similarities end here. Blomberg is unimpressed with and undaunted by the conclusions to which Ehrman's scholarship has led. There are two separate issues here. One is the credence to which Ehrman gives the lost gospels. The second is the "discredence" Ehrman gives to the Bible, including the four Gospels, based on the contradictions it allegedly contains. Blomberg's observation is helpful to pastors who may wonder if Ehrman is really on to something. He writes:

> All that is necessary is for us to have reason to believe that we can reconstruct something remarkably close to the originals [of the biblical text], and we have evidence for that in abundance. No central tenet of Christianity hangs on any textually uncertain passage; this observation alone means that Christian textual critics may examine the variants that do exist dispassionately and without worrying that their faith is somehow threatened in the ways that Ehrman came to believe.[11]

This conclusion is not surprising given that Blomberg, who received his Ph.D. from the University of Aberdeen under the supervision of esteemed scholar I. Howard Marshall, was a participant in one of the most widely respected projects on the historical reliability of the Gospels. Blomberg's 1987 volume, *The Historical Reliability of the Gospels*, was a popular summation of the six volumes titled *Gospel Perspectives*, which were published from 1980 to 1986 and address the historical reliability of the Gospels at a technical, scholarly level.[12]

There is a second evangelical scholar who emerged from a rigorous graduate program with his high view of Scripture intact. It is hard to imagine anyone whose Ph.D. program featured more impressive mentoring than what Blomberg received under the tutelage of I. Howard Marshall and what Ehrman experienced under the guidance of Bruce Metzger. But Craig Evans had the advantage of studying under multiple mentors while they were doing some of the most significant scholarly work on biblical and extrabiblical materials, including the lost gospels. Evans says that he "had the good fortune of entering Claremont Graduate University at a time when its biblical studies faculty was at its greatest."[13] James Robinson was publishing and studying the Coptic Gnostic codices found in Nag Hammadi, Egypt— the lost gospels. Burton Mack was engrossed in Philo and Jewish wisdom traditions. William Brownlee, one of the first scholars to lay eyes on the Dead Sea Scrolls, was still analyzing them. So was John Trever, the scholar who took the very first photographs of the Dead Sea Scrolls. James Sanders guided Evans through rabbinic literature and textual criticism.

So what impact did these years of rigorous scholarship under some of the tallest giants in biblical studies have upon Evans? He answers:

> I am a Christian. I was a Christian before going to seminary and graduate school, and I still am after completing school

and teaching and publishing for more than a quarter of a century. . . . My academic life has not resulted in the loss of faith . . . I realized that what biblical criticism challenged was not the essence of the Christian message, but the baggage that many think is part of the message. . . . I love to preach. I love to tell the stories of the Gospels.[14]

To be sure, anecdotal accounts of scholars neither prove nor disprove the historical reliability of the Gospels, but evangelical pastors can take comfort that a company of scholars who share the same faith journey and pursued the same academic training as Elaine Pagels and Bart Ehrman emerged with their evangelical convictions intact—even strengthened. Now we turn to some of their insights for help in framing the discussion for the listeners to whom we preach.

Know Your Skeptic

Those who preach the four Gospels should be aware of the kinds of skepticism they will encounter regarding the accounts attributed to Matthew, Mark, Luke, and John. Craig Evans is helpful here, dividing these skeptics into two schools.[15]

The first school he calls old school skeptics. These are the folks who minimize Jesus by denying the authenticity of various deeds and sayings of Jesus in the four Gospels. Evans discusses two of them—his professor James Robinson and Robert Funk, the founder of the Jesus Seminar. These two "fellows" of the Jesus Seminar met periodically with more than seventy others for several years to discuss and vote on the words of Jesus.[16] The participants used colored marbles when they voted, and a consensus was reached on each saying.

- Red means "Jesus undoubtedly said this or something very like it."
- Pink means "Jesus probably said something like this."
- Gray means "Jesus did not say this, but the ideas contained in it are close to his own."
- Black means "Jesus did not say this; it represents the perspective or content of a later tradition."

The findings were published at the end of 1993 in a volume titled *The Five Gospels: What Did Jesus Really Say?* Fewer than 20 percent of all the sayings attributed to Jesus were colored in red or pink, and more than half appeared in black!

Biblical scholars have harshly criticized the methodology and conclusions of the Jesus Seminar. Blomberg summarizes six major problems with the approach taken by the fellows involved.[17]

1. They establish far too restrictive principles for the forms of speech Jesus could have used.
2. The Seminar is equally restrictive in the topics that it permits Jesus to address.
3. The Seminar's Jesus simply is not sufficiently Jewish to be a historically credible figure.
4. There is no convincing reason left in the Seminar's Jesus for his death—death as a criminal by crucifixion.
5. After ignoring Jesus' Jewish roots, the Seminar would have us believe that later Christians re-Judaized him.
6. They are convinced that the *Gospel of Thomas* contains numerous independent traditions about the historical Jesus that are at least as reliable, if not more so, than those found in the canonical Gospels.

Two decades later, while evangelical and nonevangelical scholars disparage the work of the Jesus Seminar, its attitude toward the four Gospels has seeped into popular thinking. It certainly created a climate for a second school of skepticism. The second school, which is fueled by the contributions of Pagels and Ehrman, is what Craig Evans calls new school skeptics. These are the folks who misunderstand Jesus. According to Evans, they are "far more extreme and more radical" than the old school skeptics. This is the flavor of skepticism that is in vogue today, and one of the main personalities behind it, according to Evans, is Bart Ehrman. New school skeptics not only doubt the historical reliability of the Gospels but champion the lost gospels as a source for the kind of spirituality that is in vogue today.

Briefly the term *lost gospels* refers to the seventeen gospels found in the Nag Hammadi library. James Robinson tells the fascinating story of the discovery of these texts in his introduction to the translations of them.[18] In December 1945 two peasant brothers were digging for nitrates in the Nag Hammadi region of Upper Egypt to fertilize their crops. As they dug, Muhammed and Khalifa Ali discovered a jar and decided to smash it to find out if it contained gold. It did not. Instead, the jar contained a library consisting of twelve leather-bound books (codices) made up of papyrus pages (leaves). The books had been buried around A.D. 400. Each book (codex), except the tenth, contained a collection of tractates—shorter treatises or works. Eight pages removed from a thirteenth book were tucked inside the front cover of the sixth book. These twelve books—or thirteen counting the pages inserted into book six—contained a total of fifty-two tractates. Seventeen of these are gospels. But they are theologically unlike the four Gospels in the New Testament. Robinson observes: "The coming to light of the Nag Hammadi library gives unexpected access to the gnostic stance as Gnostics themselves presented it."[19]

Like the discovery and publication of the Qumran texts (the Dead Sea Scrolls), the discovery and publication of the Nag Hammadi library was not without drama. About a month after discovering the books, Muhammed Ali and his family brutally slaughtered the man responsible for murdering their father six months previously. This act of blood revenge prompted a police investigation, so Muhammed left the books with a Coptic priest for safekeeping. Part of the find had already been destroyed, though, as the brothers' mom had burned part of the books in her oven! Eventually, the books ended up in the hands of various neighbors and then antiquities dealers through a bartering process. Today the library is intact, housed in the Coptic Museum in Cairo, Egypt.

What to Tell Your Listeners about Textual Issues and the Lost Gospels

So what exactly should you say to your listeners—first about textual issues and second about the lost gospels? Let's begin with textual issues. Like most seminary graduates, I doubted that I would ever say anything about textual issues when I stood up to preach. The last thing nonbelieving and believing listeners need is an academic discussion about a textual variant, right? This seems self-evident, at least on the surface. Listeners do not need to see our exegetical homework, let alone our wrestling with textual critical matters. We have thirty minutes or so to "raise the dead" when we preach, and any discussion of textual issues is bound to kill a sermon. The few more sophisticated listeners who have a question about a textual variant can ask us later, right?

The problem with this line of thinking is that a couple of the more significant textual variants occur in the Gospels, namely the story of the woman caught in adultery (John 7:53–8:11) and the longer ending to Mark's Gospel (Mark 16:9–20). It is hard *not* to comment on these, lest we ignore the proverbial elephant in the room.

A few months before writing this chapter, I led a Bible study for a group that was exploring Christianity and had questions about the Bible. We worked together through the Gospel of Mark. The approach was to have people read through a section of Mark each week prior to our study and then come prepared to ask questions.

The very first question I received was from a young man who had majored in English in college and had some serious questions about the uniqueness of Christ. He asked, "Why do some manuscripts leave out 'the Son of God' in Mark 1:1?" He had simply noticed the footnote in his Bible that said: "Some manuscripts do not have *the Son of God.*" This launched us into a discussion of textual criticism, albeit in language that intelligent, bright people without a background in biblical studies could understand. If we learn to anticipate some of these objections and deal with them briefly, fairly, and honestly, we will go a long way toward building a case that the English translations we use are based on reliable manuscripts that have not been changed over the years at the whims of political or religious agendas.

But what about the lost gospels? What do our listeners need to know about them? When it is necessary to address them, the challenge is to strike a balance between economy and sufficient detail. Without bombarding our listeners with technical data, we will want to make the following points.

First, the four Gospels and the lost gospels do not come from the same historical period. As noted in an earlier chapter, New Testament scholars Carson and Moo suggest that Matthew was published shortly before A.D. 70, Mark in the late 50s or 60s, Luke in the mid or late 60s, and John somewhere between 80 and 85.[20] By contrast, the lost gospels are later, roughly between 125 and 175.[21]

Second, contrary to popular claims, the lost gospels did not gain the popularity that the four Gospels did in the early centuries of Christianity. The existing manuscripts from the second and third centuries clearly demonstrate this. Hill observes "that even in diversity-rich Egypt non-canonical Gospels were perhaps a third as popular as the canonical ones."[22]

Third, "whereas most of our early papyrus copies of the canonical Gospels are from codices which were at least suitable for the purpose of public reading in the churches, none of our surviving copies of the *Gospel of Peter* or the *Gospel of Mary* was."[23] Codices that served as "pulpit editions" were typically much larger in size, had ample margins around the writing space, were written with a more formal or regular script, and contained various kinds of markings for punctuation or division into paragraphs.[24]

Fourth, the testimony of the church fathers in the early 200s reflects consistent belief that the four Gospels—and only those four—were books of Scripture. Support comes from Hippolytus of Rome, Tertullian of Carthage, Origen of Alexandria and Caesarea, Dionysius of Alexandria, Cyprian of Carthage, and Victorinus of Pettau.[25] This flies in the face of the notion that the establishment of the canon, or accepted books of the New Testament, was imposed by Constantine in the fourth century only after being previously "up for grabs." You may want to quote from Origen (185–254) in his first homily on Luke 1:1:

I know a certain gospel which is called "The Gospel According to Thomas," and a "Gospel According to Matthias," and many others we have read—lest we should in any way be considered ignorant because of those who imagine they possess some knowledge if they are acquainted with these. Nevertheless, among all these we have approved solely what the church has recognized, which is that only the four gospels should be accepted.[26]

I have not yet mentioned the testimony of Irenaeus (ca. 130–202). Writing in about 180, he gave the impression that the church had been nurtured by the four Gospels from the time of the apostles. C. E. Hill says: "Irenaeus lies like a fallen Redwood in the path of those who would see the choice of the four Gospels as a late and politically motivated maneuver of the fourth century."[27]

Yes, Irenaeus' statement about the origins of the four Gospels in Book 3 of *Against Heresies* has become a classic:

So Matthew among the Hebrews issued a Writing of the gospel in their own tongue. . . . Mark, the disciple and interpreter of Peter, also handed down to us in writing what Peter had preached. Then Luke, the follower of Paul, recorded in a book the gospel as it was preached by him. Finally, John, the disciple of the Lord, who had also lain on his breast, himself published the Gospel, while he was residing at Ephesus in Asia.[28]

It may be worth reading this excerpt in a sermon even though some have attempted to isolate Irenaeus as a "lone voice" and as one who used faulty logic to argue for the necessity of four Gospels. As noted previously, Irenaeus was hardly a lone voice given the preponderance of testimony by the church fathers in the early third century.

Also, his well-known statement to the effect that there cannot be more or less than four Gospels due to the four winds and four zones—north, south, east, and west—cannot be dismissed as a piece of faulty logic. Rather, as Hill observes, "Irenaeus's argument is not one of logical necessity but of aesthetic necessity, of harmony, beauty, or proportion."[29]

Fifth, the content of the lost gospels is clearly contrary to the picture of Jesus in the four Gospels. Fans of the lost gospels, of course, celebrate this, but the differences are striking and disturbing to those who take seriously the authority and proclamation of the four Gospels.

For example, the *Infancy Gospel of Thomas* describes Jesus at age five making some sparrows out of mud and bringing them to life by clapping his hands after he was rebuked for making them on the Sabbath. This gospel also describes Jesus using a curse to kill a child who had bumped into him. One of the more shocking statements attributed to Jesus comes from the *Gospel of Thomas*, saying 114:

> Simon Peter said to them, "Let Mary leave us, for women are not worthy of life."

> Jesus said, "I myself shall lead her in order to make her male, so that she too may become a living spirit resembling you males. For every woman who will make herself male will enter the kingdom of heaven."[30]

Those who wish to read the lost gospels themselves will find good translations readily available in either *The Nag Hammadi Library in English,* edited by James M. Robinson, or in *Lost Scriptures: Books That Did Not Make It into the New Testament,* by Bart D. Ehrman.

Luke 1:1–4—The Confessions of a Gospel Writer

When we address the challenges posed by old school skeptics and new school skeptics, one option is to sprinkle brief comments into individual sermons on the Gospels at strategic places, but another good option is to preach an entire sermon on this matter.

Thankfully, one of the four Gospel writers took the time to describe the process in which he engaged to produce his Gospel. The preface to Luke's Gospel (1:1–4) gives us a unique window into how Luke composed his account. This is an ideal text to unpack at the beginning of a sermon series on Luke's Gospel or as a stand-alone sermon that deals with the historical reliability of the four Gospels.

Let me offer a big idea for this text: *God's spectacular plan to bring salvation to a broken world through Jesus is historically reliable.*

And here is my sermon outline:

I. Luke's Gospel is based on reliable *records* (vv. 1–2).
   A. There were many accounts—perhaps written—of Jesus' life and ministry.
   B. These accounts were handed down from eyewitnesses.
II. Luke's Gospel is based on reliable *research* (vv. 3–4).
   A. Luke's investigation was careful—as we would expect from a physician.
   B. Luke's investigation was thorough.
   C. Luke's investigation was documented.
   D. The result: we know the certainty of what we have been taught in the Gospels.

To set up this sermon, I would use the introduction to point out how God's plan for salvation, as it has been communicated in the Gospels, has been challenged by both old school skeptics (the nonhistorical Jesus movement) and new school skeptics (the lost gospels movement). I would explain how these movements influence the articles that pop up every Easter in *Time* or *Newsweek*. I would also explain how the ideas these movements stand for seep into popular culture through documentaries offered on the Discovery Channel or the History Channel. Whether intended or not, by running features on some of the more sensational claims, these articles and documentaries place novel claims and more sensible interpretations on the same level.

Toward the end of my introduction, I would raise the questions: So how can we be sure that the Bible is historically reliable? Do the Evangelists give us any assurance that what they wrote is something on which we can bank our lives?

This brings listeners to Luke's preface in 1:1–4, which is actually one beautifully written sentence in Greek. It is worth pointing out that Luke's preface "is written in a very sophisticated literary style that is reminiscent of the prefaces of the classical historians of antiquity, such as Herodotus, Thucydides, and Polybius."[31] Both I. Howard Marshall and Craig Evans find the parallel with Josephus' preface to his work *Against Apion* to be the most striking and instructive.[32] Like Josephus, Luke wants to establish the credibility of his work in case his readers are swayed by those who attempt to discredit its contents.

Some who prefer to preach deductively will share the sermon's big idea at this point. I prefer to preach this inductively, following the contours of the text and then letting the conclusion emerge at the end of the message. Before discussing the body of the sermon, it will be helpful to read through the preface.

Many have undertaken to draw up an account of the things that have been fulfilled among us, just as they were handed down to us by those who from the first were eyewitnesses and servants of the word. With this in mind, since I myself have carefully investigated everything from the beginning, I too decided to write an orderly account for you, most excellent Theophilus, so that you may know the certainty of the things you have been taught. (Luke 1:1–4)

In the body of the sermon, I unpack Luke's preface in two parts. I begin with the first half in verses 1–2, which emphasizes that Luke's Gospel is based on reliable records. In his outline of Luke's preface, Darrell Bock labels these verses "the precedents," noting that "ancient writers loved to show that what they were doing had precedents."[33] The first verb in verse 1, *epecheirēsan*, can be translated as "undertaken" or "setting the hand to" or "attempted." According to Bock, "'Setting the hand' to tell a story might well suggest written accounts here."[34] While this is not conclusive, the word choices are important. The verb *to draw up* or *compile* (*anataxasthai*) "is a technical expression of ancient historians for different kinds of recounting."[35] The object is "an account" or "a narrative" (*diēgēsis*). Though the term simply means "narrative," it is significant because it "does not refer to some form of an incomplete literary work that one could compare to the individual, detached traditions of modern form criticism."[36] Luke claims, then, for the other narrative accounts of Jesus something quite different from that envisioned by the members of the Jesus Seminar. Luke saw the prior works as narrative accounts, not a multilayered compilation of sayings that had been spliced and added to over time.

Most important, these accounts were "handed down" (*paredosan*)—a technical term for passing on official tradition[37]—by eyewitnesses. The fact that these eyewitnesses are identified by Luke as "servants of the word" at the end of verse 2 suggests that they are to be identified with the apostles. Here Marshall makes an important point against the idea that the church put words in the mouth of Jesus to serve its purposes. He argues: "Since Luke distinguishes himself and his contemporaries from them [the apostles], it follows that the content of their testimony was primarily the story of Jesus rather than of the early church."[38]

In verses 3–4, we arrive at the main clause of Luke's long sentence-preface where he describes his own role and claims that his Gospel is based on reliable research. There are at least three key points to make about Luke's research. First, his investigation was *careful*. Luke's claim that he investigated everything "carefully" (*akribōs*) is bolstered by the fact that Luke was a physician (see Col. 4:14; Philem. 24). Then, as now, physicians were intelligent folks who paid attention to detail.

Second, Luke's investigation was *thorough*. He carefully investigated "everything from the beginning." Bock makes a good case for understanding this as a reference to the beginning of what he researched—the life and ministry of Jesus—rather than simply to the beginning of his research.[39] Of course, there is no reason to doubt that the careful investigation extended to the very beginning of Luke's efforts, as well as to the beginning of the story he recounts. What an amazing opportunity Luke would have had to interview eyewitnesses around the Mediterranean world—some of whom would have been driven from Jerusalem and scattered in the Dispersion—as he accompanied the apostle Paul on his missionary journeys (see Col. 4:14; 2 Tim. 4:11; Philem. 24)! Perhaps he was able to interview Mary, the mother of Jesus, toward the end of her life!

Finally, Luke's decision to write an "orderly account"—or a "consecutive account"—tells us that his investigation was *documented*. This is self-evident, of course, from the fact that we have Luke's Gospel in our Bibles. Yet Luke's decision to write this account rather than pass it along orally adds to our confidence that we have a reliable narrative account of the life and ministry of Jesus the Messiah.

This leads to the wonderful result of Luke's narrative account that he states as his purpose in verse 4. The result is knowing the certainty of what we have been taught about Jesus in the four Gospels. The people to whom we preach—both believers and nonbelievers—need to hear the reason for our confidence that the four Gospels are historically reliable. They do not need to search elsewhere to discover "the historical Jesus." Nor do they need to fear or buy into the alternative reconstructions of what Jesus said and did. There is good reason to be confident in "the faith that was once for all entrusted to God's holy people" (Jude 3).

Staying Confident in the Face of Skepticism

The way we handle skepticism toward the four Gospels in our preaching will go a long way toward helping our listeners gain confidence and remain confident in these wonderful accounts of the words and works of Jesus. We must help our listeners understand that skepticism is not surprising. It comes with the territory.

For example, the brother of a close friend of mine is a research oncologist at one of the world's leading medical centers. He has done some ground-breaking research in the area of breast cancer, discovering a way to predict how well women will respond to drugs such as Tamoxifen. His discovery is certainly good news, and many in his field have embraced his research. Yet there are some skeptics who oppose him simply because his research does not fit the paradigm in which they have chosen to operate. Skepticism comes with the territory—both in oncology and theology.

Skepticism should not cause a loss of confidence. It is entirely expected. After all, the apostle Paul writes: "The god of this age has blinded the minds of unbelievers, so that they cannot see the light of the gospel that displays the glory of Christ, who is the image of God" (2 Cor. 4:4). This is not to mock skeptics and unbelievers. But we need to remind ourselves and our listeners that the four Gospels contain, well, gospel! God's plan for bringing salvation through the death and resurrection of Jesus the Messiah is not too good to be true. Blessed is the congregation whose pastor answers the objections of skeptics and helps them see that the four Gospels are, to quote Origen, "the pillar and foundation of the Church."[40]

CONCLUSION

How can a preacher get started with preaching the gospel from the Gospels? Whether you are a veteran pastor with twenty-five years of experience or a recent seminary graduate with decades of ministry ahead, here are some "first steps" you can take the next time you decide to do some serious preaching from the four Gospels.

1. Read and reread the Gospels.

There is no substitute for immersing ourselves in the gospel texts themselves. If you are planning on preaching through a particular Gospel, or even a part of one, then read through that Gospel several times. After two or three readings in your preferred translation, read it a couple of more times in other English translations. Read the text in Greek, too. Narrative is the easiest kind of literature to translate—even though the word *easy* may not seem appropriate here! If your Greek is rusty or on life support, at least look at a key statement or two. Use an interlinear or a Bible software program to help you.

2. Purchase a couple of the best commentaries on the Gospel you intend to preach.

I would rather have two great commentaries on a particular Gospel than five or ten good ones. If you already have a couple of great commentaries on a particular Gospel you plan to preach or repreach, then I still counsel you to buy one more you have not used before; this will give you a different "discussion partner" or mentor to challenge your thinking.

You may disagree with me on what makes a "great" commentary, but let me summarize my all-around list again. I have talked about all of these commentaries in the chapter on the correct use of Jewish and Greco-Roman background, so I here mention them only by last name.

For Matthew's Gospel, my "can't miss" list comprises Carson and France. Other fine volumes include those by Blomberg, Turner, Osborne, and, for the most detailed commentary available, the three volumes by Davies and Allison.

My list of "greats" for Mark's Gospel highlights Lane, a classic, and France. Close rivals include the commentaries by Edwards and Brooks. To dig even deeper, consult Hooker's volume.

When you turn to Luke's Gospel, it's hard to leave off Marshall's classic from the list. Bock's two volumes must stand at the head of the list, though, and some might opt to make their second commentary Green instead of Marshall. Another classic, though a bit dated, is Fitzmyer's two volumes in the Anchor Bible.

Finally, for the Gospel of John, I like Carson and the two volumes by Keener. However, Burge's volume should be considered, too; he is especially good with synthesizing the flow of the Gospel. Also, the two volumes by Brown are the forerunner to Keener in terms of detail and breadth.

3. Do some background reading in Second Temple Judaism.

Here I refer you back to chapter 3 on the correct use of Jewish and Greco-Roman background. As I suggested there, you may want to begin by reading *An Introduction to Early Judaism* by James C. VanderKam or *Exploring Jewish Literature of the Second Temple Period* by Larry Helyer. Then I would encourage you to dabble a bit in the primary sources, reading some excerpts from the five sources I recommended. This will give you a feel for religious thought during the period of the New Testament. Here are some suggestions for starters:

- Apocrypha: Sirach 1–5; Wisdom of Solomon 1–18; Tobit 1–14.

- Pseudepigrapha: *2 Baruch* 26–34; *Testament of Joseph* 19–20; *Testament of Benjamin* 1–12.

- Dead Sea Scrolls: *Manual of Discipline* (called the *Charter of a Jewish Sectarian Association* in the translation by Wise, Abegg, and Cook); *War Scroll*.

- Philo and Josephus: Philo, *Questions and Answers on Genesis II*, section 62 (on the *logos* or divine word in creation); Josephus, *The Antiquities of the Jews*, Book 18, chapter 1 and *Jewish War*, chapter 8 (on the various sects within first-century Judaism).

- Mishnah: *Shabbat* 2:5; 7:2; 8:2–3 (on the Sabbath); *Megillah* 4:1–10 (on Scripture reading in the synagogue); *Abot* 1:1–18 (on the Torah, sages, and various bits of wisdom).

As you read, ask yourself what your reading contributes to your understanding of the Jewish worldview in the first century.

What did people believe about the relationship between God and his people or about the means of salvation or the reason for suffering?

4. Select a couple of narratives and compare them in a synopsis.

Make sure you have access to a synopsis. Either dust off the one you used in seminary, purchase one, or pull up the one in your Bible software program. Whether you use a Greek only, an English only, or a Greek-English synopsis, you will find this tool indispensable for comparing and contrasting parallel accounts. Review chapter 4 on this issue to help you get started.

5. Listen to or read good sermons on the Gospels.

You can access audio and video sermons on Preaching-Today.com or on the Gospel Coalition's Web site. Chances are, your favorite preachers will have sermon series on the Gospels posted on their churches' Web sites. If they preach in a lectionary-based church, you will likely find a substantial number of sermons preached on the Gospel reading for a particular Sunday. It is worth reading sermons, too, by past and present expositors. Kent Hughes provides a compelling exposition of the Gospel of Luke in his two-volume commentary in his Preaching the Word series. Timothy Keller's recent exposition of Mark's Gospel, *King's Cross*, is a great example of how to communicate the truth of the Gospel accounts to a late-modern audience.

Love for the Gospel and the Gospel Story

Remember what Jesus said: "And this gospel of the kingdom will be preached in the whole world as a testimony to all nations, and then the end will come" (Matt. 24:14). Our task until Christ returns is to proclaim his gospel. What an urgency there is, then, to overcome the challenges we face when we tell others the story of Jesus—his works and words which bring us light and life. Our people long for this story! May God bless you, deepen your walk with Christ, deepen your congregation's walk with Christ, and expand his kingdom through you as you follow in the steps of all who sing the refrain of an old gospel song:

I love to tell the story!
'Twill be my theme in glory.
To tell the old, old story
Of Jesus and his love.[1]

THE AUTHOR

Steven D. Mathewson is senior pastor of the Evangelical Free Church of Libertyville, Illinois, and teaches preaching for the doctoral program at Denver Seminary, the master of divinity program at Trinity Evangelical Divinity School, and the undergraduates at Moody Bible Institute. He is author of *The Art of Preaching Old Testament Narrative*. He received his doctoral degree in preaching from Gordon-Conwell Theological Seminary under the mentorship of respected professor and author Haddon Robinson. He has been a pastor for more than twenty-five years and has preached sequentially through each of the four Gospels. He and his wife, Priscilla, have four grown children and two grandchildren. In his spare time, Steve enjoys fly-fishing, hiking, and watching his youngest son play college football.

NOTES

Introduction

1. The details of the story that follows come from Émile Cailliet, "The Book That Understands Me," in *A Christianity Today Reader*, ed. Frank E. Gaebelein (New York: Meredith Press, 1966), 14–17; "Émile Cailliet: The Book That Understands Me," *Eternity* 25, no. 7 (July 1974): 21–22; and Frank E. Gaebelein, "Émile Cailliet (1894–1981)," *Theology Today* 40, no. 1 (April 1983): 55–57. I first ran across Cailliet's story in Timothy Keller, *King's Cross: The Story of the World in the Life of Jesus* (New York: Dutton, 2011), xv–xvi.

2. After his conversion to Christ, Émile Cailliet eventually migrated from France to America where he served as a professor at the University of Pennsylvania, Wesleyan University, and Princeton Theological Seminary (Gaebelein, "Émile Cailliet (1894–1981)," 57.

3. This language comes from a challenge issued by D. A. Carson in *Exegetical Fallacies*, 2nd ed. (Grand Rapids: Baker, 1996), 15: "We are dealing with God's thoughts: we are obligated to take the greatest pains to understand them truly and to explain them clearly."

4. See chapter 3 for a discussion of this preacher's claim.

5. This claim comes from the character Sir Leigh Teabing in Dan Brown, *The Da Vinci Code* (New York: Doubleday, 2003), 231.

6. The phrase in quotation marks comes from the title of Dan Kimball's *They Like Jesus but Not the Church* (Grand Rapids: Zondervan, 2007).

7. This phrase comes from the title of Philip Yancey's *The Jesus I Never Knew* (Grand Rapids: Zondervan, 1995).

Chapter 1: Right Sizing

1. This phrase comes from the title of Dan Kimball's *They Like Jesus but Not the Church* (Grand Rapids: Zondervan, 2007).

2. Ibid., 37.

3. See Elaine Pagels, *Beyond Belief: The Secret Gospel of Thomas* (New York: Vintage Books, 2003); Bart D. Ehrman, *Misquoting Jesus: The Story behind Who Changed the Bible and Why* (San Francisco: HarperSanFrancisco, 2005); and Bart D. Ehrman, *Lost Scriptures: Books That Did Not Make It into the New Testament* (New York: Oxford University Press, 2003). The story about the boy Jesus lengthening the board appears in the Infancy Gospel of Thomas 13:1–2. Several good evangelical assessments of the "lost gospels" are available. Two of the most helpful are Craig A. Evans, *Fabricating Jesus: How Modern Scholars Distort the Gospels* (Downers Grove, IL: InterVarsity, 2006); and C. E. Hill, *Who Chose the Gospels? Probing the Great Gospel Conspiracy* (New York: Oxford University Press, 2010).

4. Gary M. Burge, *John*, The NIV Application Commentary (Grand Rapids: Zondervan, 2000), 41.

5. Ibid.

6. David L. Turner, *Matthew*, Baker Exegetical Commentary on the New Testament (Grand Rapids: Baker Academic, 2008), 9–10.

7. The outline I have presented uses simple chapter divisions. For the exact chapter and verse divisions, see D. A. Carson, "Matthew," in *Matthew and Mark*, The Expositor's Bible Commentary, rev. ed., vol. 9 (Grand Rapids: Zondervan, 2010), 77–84; Turner, *Matthew*, vii–viii, 8–10.

8. Turner, *Matthew*, 9.

9. Craig L. Blomberg, *Matthew*, The New American Commentary (Nashville: Broadman, 1992), 49.

10. William L. Lane, *The Gospel according to Mark*, The New International Commentary on the New Testament (Grand Rapids: Eerdmans, 1974).

11. R. T. France, *The Gospel of Mark*, The New International Greek Testament Commentary (Grand Rapids: Eerdmans, 2002), vii–viii. The heading and prologue (1:1–13) would obviously be incorporated into the first series.

12. Darrell L. Bock, *Luke*, Baker Exegetical Commentary on the New Testament (Grand Rapids: Baker Academic, 1994), 1:43–48. Cf. I. Howard Marshall, *The Gospel of Luke*, The New International Greek Testament Commentary (Grand Rapids: Eerdmans, 1978), 7–11; and Joel B. Green, *The Gospel of Luke*, The New International Commentary on the New Testament (Grand Rapids: Eerdmans, 1997), 25–29.

13. Timothy Keller's chapter titles could work as sermon titles: "The People around Jesus," "The Two Lost Sons," "Redefining Sin," "Redefining Lostness," "The True Elder Brother," "Redefining Hope," and "The Feast of the Father." See *The Prodigal God* (New York: Dutton, 2008), vii–ix.

14. David E. Garland groups these stories together in *Mark,* The NIV Application Commentary (Grand Rapids: Zondervan, 1996), 475–86.

15. Adapted and summarized from Haddon W. Robinson, *Biblical Preaching: The Development and Delivery of Expository Messages*, 2nd ed. (Grand Rapids: Baker Academic, 2001), 75–96, 102–3.

16. Reg Grant, "The Public Expository Reading of Scripture" (RHMA Church Planting Conference, Morton, IL, April 25, 1992).

17. Max McLean made this statement and those that follow in a doctoral seminar in preaching at Gordon-Conwell Theological Seminary (Charlotte, NC, campus, January 26, 1998).

Chapter 2: Are Jesus and Paul on the Same Page?

1. I. Howard Marshall, *New Testament Theology: One Gospel, Many Witnesses* (Downers Grove, IL: InterVarsity, 2004), 474.

2. See D. A. Carson and Douglas J. Moo, *An Introduction to the New Testament*, 2nd ed. (Grand Rapids: Zondervan, 2005), 156, 182,

210, 267, 394, 448, 464, 487, 507, 522, 543–44, 572, 578, 583, 592, 608, 626, 646, 663, 676, 692, 707, 712. They suggest Matthew was published shortly before A.D. 70, Mark in the late 50s or 60s, Luke in the mid or late 60s, and John between 80 and 85. As for the Pauline Epistles, Carson and Moo date Romans around A.D. 57, 1 Corinthians ca. 55, 2 Corinthians ca. 56–57, Galatians ca. 48, Ephesians in the early 60s, Philippians between the mid-50s and early 60s, Colossians in the late 50s or early 60s, 1 Thessalonians in 50, 2 Thessalonians in late 50 or early 51, 1 Timothy in the mid-50s or mid-60s, 2 Timothy ca. 64–65, Titus between the late 50s and middle 60s, and Philemon in the early 60s. As for the General Epistles, Carson and Moo date Hebrews prior to 70, James in the early or mid-40s, 1 Peter in 62–63, 2 Peter shortly before 65, the three Epistles of John in the early 90s, Jude in the mid to late 60s, and Revelation ca. 95–96.

3. Marshall, *New Testament Theology*, 580. Marshall makes this point in reference to the Synoptic Gospels, but it certainly applies to the Gospel of John as well.

4. Scot McKnight, "Jesus vs. Paul," *Christianity Today*, December 2010, 26.

5. Ibid.

6. Marshall, *New Testament Theology*, 483. A few pages earlier, he says that Paul shares the same gospel as other early Christians (1 Cor. 15:3–5), 471.

7. McKnight, "Jesus vs. Paul," 28. The italics are McKnight's.

8. The reference is Luke 18:14 where Jesus speaks first about the humble tax collector and then a proud Pharisee: "I tell you that this man, rather than the other, went home justified before God." Other possible references include Matthew 12:37, Luke 10:29, and Luke 16:16. In the latter two, Jesus uses "justified" more in the sense of personal, self-justification rather than a forensic declaration as in Paul. In Matthew 12:37, Jesus' saying is more proverbial than forensic.

9. Marshall, *New Testament Theology*, 476.

10. Ibid.

11. McKnight, "Jesus vs. Paul," 28.

12. Marshall, *New Testament Theology*, 579.

13. Gordon D. Fee, *1 and 2 Timothy, Titus: A Good News Commentary* (San Francisco: Harper & Row, 1984), xix.

14. Marshall, *New Testament Theology*, 593.

15. Ibid., 474.

16. Marshall's comments on the differences between the Paul of Acts and the Paul of the Letters apply here (ibid., 485).

17. Ibid., 486.

18. Ibid., 487.

19. D. A. Carson, *Jesus' Sermon on the Mount and His Confrontation with the World: An Exposition of Matthew 5–10* (Grand Rapids: Baker, 1999), 140.

20. Ibid., 143–44.

21. David L. Turner, *Matthew*, Baker Exegetical Commentary on the New Testament (Grand Rapids: Baker Academic, 2008), 213.

22. Ibid., 220.

23. D. A. Carson, "Matthew," in *Matthew and Mark*, The Expositor's Bible Commentary, rev. ed., vol. 9 (Grand Rapids: Zondervan, 2010), 586.

24. Grant R. Osborne, *Matthew*, Zondervan Exegetical Commentary on the New Testament (Grand Rapids: Zondervan, 2010), 723.

25. Carson, "Matthew," 479.

26. The Greek phrase is ὑπακοὴν πίστεως (*hypakoēn pisteōs*). The term πίστεως (*pisteōs*, faith) can be read as a subjective genitive emphasizing the source ("obedience which comes from faith") or an epexegetic genitive equating the two ("obedience which is faith").

27. Douglas Moo, *The Epistle to the Romans*, The New International Commentary on the New Testament (Grand Rapids: Eerdmans, 1996), 52–53.

28. Simon Gathercole, "What Did Paul Really Mean?" *Christianity Today*, August 2007, 24.

29. Carson and Moo, *Introduction to the New Testament*, 380.

30. Gathercole, "What Did Paul Really Mean?" 26. Cf. Carson and Moo, *Introduction to the New Testament*, 380.

31. See the comprehensive study of key Second Temple texts in D. A. Carson, Peter T. O'Brien, Mark A. Seifrid, eds., *Justification and Variegated Nomism*, vol. 1, *The Complexities of Second Temple Judaism*

(Grand Rapids: Baker Academic, 2001). The volume concludes that works-righteousness was, in fact, one of the beliefs prevalent in Second Temple Judaism, regardless of what was said about election and grace.

32. This translation is from James H. Charlesworth, ed., *The Old Testament Pseudepigrapha*, vol. 2 (New York: Doubleday, 1985), 660. For a discussion of the date, see ibid., 640–41; and Larry R. Helyer, *Exploring Jewish Literature of the Second Temple Period* (Downers Grove, IL: InterVarsity, 2002), 389.

33. This translation is from James H. Charlesworth, ed., *The Old Testament Pseudepigrapha*, vol. 1 (New York: Doubleday, 1983), 638. For a discussion of the date, see ibid., 616–17; and Helyer, *Exploring Jewish Literature*, 423.

34. This translation is from H. St. J. Thackeray, trans., *Josephus,* vol. 1, *The Life* and *Against Apion* in the Loeb Classical Library (Cambridge, MA: Harvard University Press, 1926), 381. For a discussion of the date, see Helyer, *Exploring Jewish Literature*, 347.

35. See D. A. Carson, "Summaries and Conclusions," in Carson, O'Brien, and Seifrid, *Justification and Variegated Nomism*, vol. 1, 543–48.

36. See McKnight, "Jesus vs. Paul," 26.

37. Marshall, *New Testament Theology*, 601.

Chapter 3: Background Check

1. David Van Biema, "Re-Judaizing Jesus," *Time*, March 24, 2008, 60.

2. As quoted in ibid.

3. Rob Bell, *Velvet Elvis: Repainting the Christian Faith* (Grand Rapids: Zondervan, 2005), 128.

4. Ibid., 127.

5. Ibid., 129.

6. Ibid., 132.

7. Ben Witherington, "Velvet Elvis and the King"—Has He Left the Building?" *Ben Witherington* (blog), February 17, 2007, http://benwitherington.blogspot.com/2007/02/velvet-elvis-and-king-has-he-left.html.

8. Ben Witherington, "Rob Bell Hits Lexington and a Packed-Out House," *Ben Witherington* (blog), February 15, 2007, http://benwitherington.blogspot.com/2007/02/rob-bell-hits-lexington-and-packedout.html.

9. Bell, *Velvet Elvis*, 189, note 98.

10. Ibid., 132.

11. Ibid.

12. D. A. Carson, "Matthew," in *Matthew and Mark*, The Expositor's Bible Commentary, rev. ed., vol. 9 (Grand Rapids: Zondervan, 2010), 420–21; Donald A. Hagner, *Matthew 14–28*, Word Biblical Commentary, vol. 33b (Dallas: Word Books, 1995), 471; Craig S. Keener, *The Gospel of Matthew: A Socio-Rhetorical Commentary* (Grand Rapids: Eerdmans, 2009), 428.

13. Keener, *Matthew*, 424; Hagner, *Matthew 14–28*, 471–72.

14. Hagner points out that some commentators see the metaphor as extending to evil spiritual forces. He comments: "There is risk in some of these more adventuresome proposals, yet since the ultimate survival of the church is in view, certainly the ultimate defeat of all evil is at least implied." *Matthew 14–28*, 472.

15. Ben Witherington III, *Matthew*, Smyth & Helwys Bible Commentary (Macon: Smyth & Helwys Publishing, 2006), 318.

16. Ibid., 316.

17. The expression "Second Temple Judaism" refers to Judaism between the completion of the second temple in Jerusalem in 516 B.C. (Solomon's temple being the first) to its destruction in A.D. 70. I will use the term as do New Testament scholars when they employ it as a kind of shorthand for Judaism in Jesus' day, that is, in the first century A.D.

18. Rob Bell has a fine discussion of this, too, in a note in *Velvet Elvis* (192, note 140). I point this out for two reasons. First, people like Rob Bell and Ray Vander Laan do get some details right! Second, the best way to evaluate them is to read the best commentaries. If Bell or Vander Laan or anyone else offers a legitimate insight, it is likely that one of the best commentators has already discussed it. This is not to disparage Bell or Vander Laan or anyone else. It is simply to point out the need to rely on a community of scholars who have given their lives

to studying every aspect of the text, including its historical-cultural background.

19. Craig S. Keener is the editor of *The IVP Bible Background Commentary: New Testament* (Downers Grove, IL: InterVarsity, 1993). This volume is useful, but pastors who have Keener's commentaries on Matthew and John, as well as good commentaries on Mark and Luke by other authors, will probably find nothing new in it.

20. William L. Lane, *The Gospel of Mark*, The New International Commentary on the New Testament (Grand Rapids: Eerdmans, 1974), 42.

21. Ibid., 43.

22. Darrell L. Bock, *Luke 1:1–9:50*, Baker Exegetical Commentary on the New Testament (Grand Rapids: Baker Academic, 1994), 213.

23. Ibid., 214.

24. D. A. Carson, *The Gospel according to John*, The Pillar New Testament Commentary (Grand Rapids: Eerdmans, 1990), 321–29; Gary M. Burge, *John*, The NIV Application Commentary (Grand Rapids: Zondervan, 2000), 219–21, 226–29.

25. Burge, *John*, 221.

26. Carson, *John*, 321–22.

27. Craig S. Keener, *The Gospel of John: A Commentary* (Peabody, MA: Hendrickson, 2003), 1:185–94.

28. Personal conversation with Craig Blomberg, July 29, 2010.

29. Craig L. Blomberg, *A Handbook of New Testament Exegesis* (Grand Rapids: Baker Academic, 2010), 75 (especially note 35).

30. Personal correspondence with David Turner, December 1, 2010.

31. The label *Apocrypha* dates to the time of Jerome in the fourth century. The reason for this label is uncertain, and the label itself is unhelpful. The actual number of books or parts of books belonging to this collection is disputed since the three major Greek codices—Vaticanus, Sinaiticus, and Alexandrinus—of the Septuagint (LXX) contain them in various numbers and together contain four more books or parts of books than found in the Roman Catholic Canon (see D. A. Carson and Douglas J. Moo, *An Introduction to the New Testament*, 2nd ed. [Grand

Rapids: Zondervan, 2005], 730; see also "The Names and Order of the Books" at the beginning of the New Revised Standard Version of the Bible). For a discussion of why evangelicals, and Protestants in general, do not recognize the apocryphal books as Scripture, see Carson and Moo, *Introduction to the New Testament*, 730–31 or F. F. Bruce, *The Canon of Scripture* (Downers Grove, IL: InterVarsity, 1988), 68–97.

32. A commentator, Darrell L. Bock, tipped me off to the appropriate reference in the Apocrypha. See *Luke 9:51–24:53*, Baker Exegetical Commentary on the New Testament (Grand Rapids: Baker Academic, 1996), 979–80; cf. Darrell L. Bock, *Luke*, The NIV Application Commentary (Grand Rapids: Zondervan, 1996), 285.

33. Ben Witherington III, *Jesus the Sage: The Pilgrimage of Wisdom* (Minneapolis: Fortress Press, 2000), 158–59. Cf. Robert H. Stein, *The Method and Message of Jesus' Teaching*, rev. ed. (Louisville: Westminster John Knox, 1994), 2–3.

34. Larry R. Helyer, *Exploring Jewish Literature of the Second Temple Period* (Downers Grove, IL: InterVarsity, 2002), 21.

35. An older edition, edited by R. H. Charles in 1913, is also still available. It covers both the Apocrypha and the Pseudepigrapha. But Charlesworth's volumes have become the standard editions.

36. A lecture by Gary M. Burge provided this connection, and he discusses it as well in *John*, 197.

37. Carson, *John*, 149–50.

38. Michael Wise, Martin Abegg, Jr., and Edward Cook, *The Dead Sea Scrolls: A New Translation*, rev. ed. (San Francisco: HarperOne, 2005), 11.

39. Ibid., 13.

40. The traditional view attributes the origins of the Dead Sea Scrolls (hereafter DSS) to the Essenes. This view is appealing because the description of the Essenes by Josephus corresponds to details in a Dead Sea text known variously as the *Manual of Discipline*, the *Community Rule*, or the *Charter of a Jewish Sectarian Association*. (Wise, Abegg, and Cook, *Dead Sea Scrolls*, 15). However, Wise, Abegg, and Cook (25–26) challenge this because of several discrepancies: (1) Philo describes the Essenes as celibate, yet numerous passages in the DSS presuppose

the marriage of group members; (2) Philo describes the Essenes as pursuing only peaceful occupation, yet the *War Scroll* gives prescriptions for an armed conflict, albeit future, against the powers of darkness; (3) Philo and Josephus indicate that the Essenes rejected slavery, yet the *Damascus Document* has rules governing the treatment of slaves, while the *Ordinances* further regulates slavery; (4) Josephus mentions the white garments of the Essenes, while the DSS say nothing about this; (5) neither Josephus nor Philo says anything about the Essenes following a 364-day solar calendar that was a key tenet of the community producing the DSS; (6) the DSS emphasize the role of priests in the group's leadership, yet Josephus says nothing about this even though he came from a priestly family and claimed to have studied with the Essenes as a youth; and (7) Josephus says nothing about the Teacher of Righteousness, a prominent figure in the sectarian portions of the DSS. Instead, Wise, Abegg, and Cook (31) propose that the DSS are the product of a diverse movement that resembles the Sadducees in some ways and the Essenes in others. "This movement was clearly favorable to priests, inclined to support those rulers who submitted to priestly direction, and was violently averse to Pharisaism—perhaps because that ideology allowed lay teachers, the later rabbis, to revise traditional laws. The movement arose among the religious conservatives of its day, whereas the Pharisees were more liberal" (33). Yet Larry Helyer defends the Essene hypothesis, noting that Pliny described the Essenes as living on the west shore of the Dead Sea, north of Engedi and Masada, and that Josephus was aware of two groups of Essenes, one celibate and the other not (*Exploring Jewish Literature*, 194). Fortunately, the exact identification of the sect responsible for producing, copying, and safe keeping the scrolls is not essential for reading and interpreting them.

41. Personal correspondence with Weston W. Fields, November 28, 2009. Fields noted that all three editions were done before the official publication of some of the texts and that some of the texts are still not published.

42. Helyer, *Exploring Jewish Literature*, 201–6.

43. See ibid., 207. Compare the *Damascus Document* 6:14–21 with Jesus' words in Matt. 23; Mark 7:10–11; 12:40; Luke 20:47.

44. Helyer, *Exploring Jewish Literature*, 22.

45. The Loeb Classical Library covers the works of Philo in eleven volumes and the works of Josephus in thirteen (nine for *Jewish Antiquities*, three for *Jewish War*, and one for *The Life* and *Against Apion*).

46. See Philo, *On Flight and Finding*, 101 (*The Works of Philo*, trans. C. D. Yonge [Peabody, MA: Hendrickson, 1993], 330) and *Questions and Answers on Genesis, II*, 62 (Yonge, *Works of Philo*), 834.

47. See Josephus, *The Antiquities of the Jews*, Books 14–17 on Herod. Particularly relevant passages about Herod's violence occur in 15.7; 16.11; 17.7–8.

48. Helyer, *Exploring Jewish Literature*, 451–52.

49. Jacob Neusner, *The Mishnah: A New Translation* (New Haven, CT: Yale University Press, 1988), xv.

50. Jacob Neusner, *Judaism when Christianity Began* (Louisville: Westminster John Knox, 2002), 7.

51. Ibid., 8.

52. Carson, *Matthew*, 58.

53. A reasonably priced paperback edition of this volume has recently been released by Hendrickson Publishers.

54. Helyer, *Exploring Jewish Literature*, 451.

55. Bock, *Luke 1:1–9:50*, 403, note 18.

56. D. A. Carson, *Exegetical Fallacies*, 2nd ed. (Grand Rapids: Baker Academic, 1996), 15.

Chapter 4: Conflicting Reports?

1. Scot McKnight lists and discusses "seven important characteristics" of editorial activity in the Synoptic Gospels in *Interpreting the Synoptic Gospels* (Grand Rapids: Baker, 1988), 85–87.

2. Ibid., 86. McKnight continues: "When it comes to the sayings of Jesus, students will want to decide whether Jesus repeated himself in two different settings or whether the Evangelists have chosen to transpose a saying from one setting to another. To rule out either option at the outset is to prejudge the matter."

3. G. R. Osborne, "Redaction Criticism," in *Dictionary of Jesus and the Gospels*, ed. Joel B. Green, Scot McKnight, and I. Howard Marshall (Downers Grove, IL: InterVarsity, 1992), 662.

4. See ibid.," 662–64 for a helpful discussion of both the relationship of redaction criticism to other schools of criticism and also redaction criticism's origin.

5. D. A. Carson, "Redaction Criticism: On the Legitimacy and Illegitimacy of a Literary Tool," in *Scripture and Truth*, ed. D. A. Carson and John D. Woodbridge (Grand Rapids: Zondervan, 1983), 126.

6. Ibid., 127.

7. Osborne, "Redaction Criticism," 668.

8. Doris Kearns Goodwin, *Team of Rivals: The Political Genius of Abraham Lincoln* (New York: Simon & Schuster, 2006), xvi.

9. Douglas L. Wilson, *Lincoln's Sword: The Presidency and the Power of Words* (New York: Alfred A. Knopf, 2006), 3.

10. Carson, "Redaction Criticism," 126.

11. See the discussion in Craig L. Blomberg, *The Historical Reliability of the Gospels,* 2nd ed. (Downers Grove, IL: InterVarsity, 2007), 157–68.

12. Blomberg, *Historical Reliability*, 157.

13. Carson, "Redaction Criticism," 130.

14. Craig A. Evans, *Luke*, New International Biblical Commentary (Peabody, MA: Hendrickson, 1990), 151. See also Darrell L. Bock, *Luke 9:51–24:53*, Baker Exegetical Commentary on the New Testament (Grand Rapids: Baker Academic, 1996), 866. Bock believes that Luke 9:33 rejects this Feast of Booths/Tabernacles connection. However, Bock gives no substantial explanation as to how Luke 9:33 rejects the connection. Obviously Luke 9:33 criticizes Peter's misinterpretation of this event. But the misinterpretation may have to do with Peter's desire to prolong the experience rather than with Peter's association of this experience with the Feast of Booths or Tabernacles. So, then, Luke 9:33 does not necessarily rule out Luke making a legitimate connection (with his "about eight days later" reference) between the transfiguration and a sacred assembly that took place on the eighth day of the Feast of Booths.

15. Evans, *Luke*, 151.

16. For a helpful discussion of Luke's portrait of Jesus at prayer, see Joel B. Green, *The Theology of the Gospel of Luke* (Cambridge: Cambridge University Press, 1995), 58–60.

17. I. Howard Marshall, *The Gospel of Luke*, The New International Greek Testament Commentary (Grand Rapids: Eerdmans, 1978), 177.

18. Ibid.

19. Ibid., 178.

20. The description of Matthew 8:1–9:34 as an anthology of Jesus' works of power comes from R. T. France, *The Gospel of Matthew*, The New International Commentary on the New Testament (Grand Rapids: Eerdmans, 2007), 299–300.

21. Ibid., 333.

22. Personal translation of the Greek text of 8:22a. The NIV and ESV render the opening words of the account as "One day."

23. Darrell L. Bock, *Jesus according to Scripture: Restoring the Portrait from the Gospels* (Grand Rapids: Baker, 2002), 211.

24. McKnight offers a helpful distinction between a harmony and a synopsis: "In general, a harmony presents the same event or saying in the life of Jesus from the Gospels in parallel fashion so that the reader can easily harmonize events and sayings. Harmonies are almost always based upon a given chronology of the life of Jesus. Synopses, on the other hand, place parallel accounts of the same event or saying side by side so that the reader can compare similarities and dissimilarities word by word. Thus, whereas a harmony is normally concerned with constructing a life of Jesus by facilitating a broad comparison of *events*, the intention of a synopsis is the careful comparison of *words*" (*Interpreting the Synoptic Gospels*, 40–41). Currently, the best harmony is Robert L. Thomas and Stanley N. Gundry, *A Harmony of the Gospels* (New York: Harper Collins, 1986). This edition is based on the New American Standard Bible and is a reprint of a 1978 edition originally published by Moody Press. Robert L. Thomas and Stanley N. Gundry have also published *The NIV Harmony of the Gospels* (New York: HarperCollins, 1988).

25. For a helpful discussion by a conservative evangelical of harmonization as an apologetic tool, see Craig L. Blomberg, "The Legitimacy

and Limits of Harmonization," in *Hermeneutics, Authority, and Canon,* ed. D. A. Carson and John D. Woodbridge (Grand Rapids: Zondervan, 1986), 135–74.

26. These synopses can be purchased online through the American Bible Society or leading book distributors such as Amazon or Christian Book Distributors. Seminary bookstores carry these resources as well.

27. For a thorough discussion of this aspect of exegesis, see chap. 3 in this volume.

28. See McKnight, *Interpreting the Synoptic Gospels,* 42–43. I have followed McKnight's scheme except that I use purple for words that are totally unparalleled—that is, not found in either of the other Synoptic Gospels. McKnight does not underline unparalleled words. The beauty of using McKnight's scheme is that preachers can check their underlining for accuracy by comparing it with W. R. Farmer, *Synopticon* (Cambridge: Cambridge University Press, 1969). The price and availability of Farmer's volume may mean that it is accessible only to pastors who live in a community with a seminary library or a university library with a significant biblical studies collection.

29. See D. A. Carson, "Matthew," in *Matthew and Mark,* The Expositor's Bible Commentary, rev. ed., vol. 9 (Grand Rapids: Zondervan, 2010), 326.

30. Bock, *Jesus according to Scripture,* 50.

31. Ibid.

Chapter 5: Dealing with Darkness

1. This account is contained in Luke 8:26–39.

2. Clinton E. Arnold, *Three Crucial Questions about Spiritual Warfare* (Grand Rapids: Baker, 1997), 101–3, 207. Arnold notes that a group of psychologists proposed the inclusion of a new diagnostic category called "Trance and Possession Disorder" (TPD) in the fourth edition of the *Diagnostic and Statistical Manual of Mental Disorders* (*DSM-IV*), yet this proposal was ultimately rejected.

3. Haddon W. Robinson, "A Case Study in Temptation," in *Biblical Sermons,* ed. Haddon W. Robinson (Grand Rapids: Baker, 1989), 22.

4. The course was THS 661 Equipping for Spiritual Warfare, at Western Seminary in the summer of 1998. It was taught by Gerry Breshears, to whom I am indebted for shaping my biblical understanding of spiritual warfare. Clinton E. Arnold's previously mentioned book, *Three Crucial Questions about Spiritual Warfare*, was also formative.

5. Peter Wagner uses the expression "ley lines" in his book *Breaking Strongholds*, but he doesn't define it. I understand his use of the phrase to mean that ley lines are streams or currents of supernatural energy that supposedly run between and connect places with prominent sources of magical or spiritual power. These places might be the sites of military battles, occult activity, gambling, or prostitution. In some cases, these places might be cities.

6. I am indebted to Gerry Breshears and his unpublished handout "Three Models of Deliverance" for identifying and labeling these three categories.

7. Grant R. Osborne, *Matthew*, Zondervan Exegetical Commentary on the New Testament (Grand Rapids: Zondervan, 2010).

8. Ibid., 128.

9. Ibid., 136.

10. For a fuller discussion, see Mark Driscoll and Gerry Breshears, *Vintage Church* (Wheaton, IL: Crossway, 2008), 282–83.

11. Personal conversation with Gerry Breshears, May 25, 2011.

12. Craig L. Blomberg, *Matthew*, The New American Commentary (Nashville: Broadman, 1992); William W. Klein, Craig L. Blomberg, and Robert L. Hubbard, Jr., *Introduction to Biblical Interpretation*, rev. ed. (Nashville: Thomas Nelson, 2004).

13. Personal correspondence with Craig L. Blomberg, May 24, 2011.

14. Ibid.

15. Personal conversation with Gerry Breshears, May 25, 2011.

16. Arnold, *Three Crucial Questions*, 80.

17. Ibid., 79.

18. Ibid., 80.

19. Ibid. Arnold cites Romans 5:1 to note that God legally acquits us from our guilt due to sin and Colossians 1:13 to note that believers are transferred from Satan's domain into God's kingdom.

20. Ibid.

21. Ibid., 81–82.

22. See Ibid., 73–141 for a complete discussion of this issue.

23. Personal conversation with Grant Osborne, June 9, 2011.

24. Haddon Robinson, "The Heresy of Application," in *The Art and Craft of Biblical Preaching,* ed. Haddon Robinson and Brian Larson (Grand Rapids: Zondervan, 2005), 308.

25. Personal conversation with Grant Osborne, June 9, 2011.

26. Arnold, *Three Crucial Questions*, 21.

27. This language comes from Hal Lindsey's popular book *Satan Is Alive and Well on Planet Earth* (1972).

28. Darrell L. Bock, *Luke,* The NIV Application Commentary (Grand Rapids: Zondervan, 1996), 244.

Chapter 6: On Purpose

1. "Mexican Drug Cartel Co-opts Springs Writer's Message," *The Gazette*, Colorado Springs, June 25, 2010.

2. Haddon Robinson, "The Heresy of Application," in *The Art and Craft of Biblical Preaching,* ed. Haddon Robinson and Craig Brian Larson (Grand Rapids: Zondervan, 2005), 306.

3. David Jackman, "The Hermeneutical Distinctives of Expository Preaching," in *Preach the Word: Essays on Expository Preaching in Honor of R. Kent Hughes*, ed. Leland Ryken and Todd Wilson (Wheaton, IL: Crossway, 2007), 18.

4. Daniel M. Doriani, *Putting the Truth to Work: The Theory and Practice of Biblical Application* (Phillipsburg, NJ: P & R, 2001), vii.

5. This comes from the title of a book by a fine preacher and author. See John Ortberg, *If You Want to Walk on Water, You've Got to Get Out of the Boat* (Grand Rapids: Zondervan, 2001).

6. William W. Klein, Craig L. Blomberg, and Robert L. Hubbard, Jr., *Introduction to Biblical Interpretation*, rev. ed. (Nashville: Thomas Nelson, 2004), 477–504. I single out Blomberg because he is responsible for much of the material in this volume on application, particularly related to the four Gospels.

7. Doriani, *Putting the Truth to Work*, x.

8. Ibid., 82. See pp. 82–92 for an explication of these seven ways.

9. Steven D. Mathewson, *The Art of Preaching Old Testament Narrative* (Grand Rapids: Baker Academic, 2002), 23–24.

10. Klein, Blomberg, and Hubbard, *Introduction to Biblical Interpretation*, 401.

11. Sidney Greidanus, *The Modern Preacher and the Ancient Text: Interpreting and Preaching Biblical Literature* (Grand Rapids: Eerdmans, 1988), 295–96. Greidanus also writes: "Summarizing, we can say that all the Gospel writers intend to write their good news about Jesus Christ in a historical way; that is, they related actual historical events to proclaim their good news" (277).

12. Gordon D. Fee and Douglas Stuart, *How to Read the Bible for All Its Worth,* 3rd ed. (Grand Rapids: Zondervan, 2003), 105–6.

13. Craig L. Blomberg, *Neither Poverty nor Riches: A Biblical Theology of Material Possessions* (Grand Rapids: Eerdmans, 1999), 163.

14. Doriani, *Putting the Truth to Work*, 194.

15. Ibid., 197.

16. Ibid., 199.

17. Ibid., 88.

18. See Klein, Blomberg, and Hubbard, *Introduction to Biblical Interpretation*, 490.

19. Ibid., 491.

20. See Philip J. King and Lawrence E. Stager, *Life in Biblical Israel* (Louisville: Westminster John Knox Press, 2001), 24.

21. Doriani, *Putting the Truth to Work*, 184.

22. George Eldon Ladd, *The Gospel of the Kingdom* (Grand Rapids: Eerdmans, 1959), 42.

23. Doriani, *Putting the Truth to Work*, 201–2.

24. Ibid., 202.

25. Ibid.

26. Ortberg, *If You Want to Walk*, 16–17.

27. Grant R. Osborne, *Matthew*, Zondervan Exegetical Commentary on the New Testament (Grand Rapids: Zondervan, 2010), 577–78.

28. Ibid., 578.

29. Klein, Blomberg, and Hubbard, *Introduction to Biblical Interpretation*, 488–89.

30. Commentators note that the sword is clearly metaphorical as indicated by Jesus' "That is enough," in Luke 22:38. Joel B. Green understands this as "an expression of exasperation." *The Gospel of Luke*, The New International Commentary on the New Testament (Grand Rapids: Eerdmans, 1997), 775. Darrell L. Bock sees Jesus' words as "a Semitic expression that means he is dismissing the topic" due to the disciples' misunderstanding. *Luke 9:51–24:53*, Baker Exegetical Commentary on the New Testament (Grand Rapids: Baker Academic, 1996), 1749.

31. Green, *The Gospel of Luke*, 774. To be sure, the seventy-two were prepped to encounter resistance. After all, Jesus said, "I am sending you out like lambs among wolves" (Luke 10:3). Yet the seventy-two returned with joy, testifying that even the demons submitted to them in Jesus' name (Luke 10:17). So the climate they encountered was certainly more favorable than the one Jesus anticipates in Luke 22:35–38.

32. Doriani, *Putting the Truth to Work*, 205–6.

33. Jack Kuhatschek, *Taking the Guesswork Out of Applying the Bible* (Grand Rapids: Zondervan, 1990), 149.

34. Doriani, *Putting the Truth to Work*, 185.

35. Ibid.

36. Ibid., 187.

Chapter 7: Against Counterfeits

1. Dan Brown, *The Da Vinci Code* (New York: Doubleday, 2003), 231.

2. Ibid., 235.

3. Elaine Pagels, *Beyond Belief: The Secret Gospel of Thomas* (New York: Vintage, 2003), 30.

4. Ibid., 32.

5. Ibid.

6. Ibid., 68.

7. Bart D. Ehrman, *Jesus, Interrupted: Revealing the Hidden Contradictions in the Bible (and Why We Don't Know about Them)* (San

Francisco: HarperOne, 2009), ix. This detail and the details that follow come from the Preface (ix–xii).

8. Ibid., xi.

9. See Bart D. Ehrman, *Lost Christianities: The Battle for Scripture and the Faiths We Never Knew* (New York: Oxford University Press, 2003), 1–8.

10. See Craig L. Blomberg, review of *Misquoting Jesus: The Story Behind Who Changed the Bible and Why* by Bart D. Ehrman, *Denver Journal* 9 (2006), http://www.denverseminary.edu/the-denver-journal/2006/.

11. Ibid. Blomberg also offers one of the most helpful answers I have ever read to the question (or objection) as to why God did not allow the original manuscripts, which evangelicals believe were without error (inerrant), to be copied without error down through the centuries. This is one of Ehrman's issues with the doctrine of inerrancy. If God had inspired the originals, Ehrman contends, he could have and should have preserved them without error. Blomberg responds: "It would have been a far greater miracle to supernaturally guide every copyist and translator throughout history than to inspire one set of original authors, and in the process it probably would have violated the delicate balance between the humanity and divinity of the Bible analogous to the humanity and divinity of Christ."

12. Craig L. Blomberg, *The Historical Reliability of the Gospels* (Downers Grove, IL: InterVarsity, 1987), xi–xii.

13. Craig A. Evans, *Fabricating Jesus: How Modern Scholars Distort the Gospels* (Downers Grove, IL: InterVarsity, 2006), 9.

14. Ibid., 12–13.

15. Ibid., 21–31.

16. The details that follow come from Craig L. Blomberg, "Where Do We Start Studying Jesus?" in *Jesus under Fire: Modern Scholarship Reinvents the Historical Jesus*, ed. Michael J. Wilkins and J. P. Moreland (Grand Rapids: Zondervan, 1995), 18–19.

17. Ibid., 20–23.

18. James M. Robinson, "Introduction," in *The Nag Hammadi Library in English*, rev. ed., ed. James M. Robinson (San Francisco: HarperSanFrancisco, 1990), 10–26.

19. Ibid., 3.

20. D. A. Carson and Douglas J. Moo, *An Introduction to the New Testament*, 2nd ed. (Grand Rapids: Zondervan, 2005), 156, 182, 210, 267.

21. See C. E. Hill, *Who Chose the Gospels? Probing the Great Gospel Conspiracy* (Oxford: Oxford University Press, 2010), 7–9.

22. Ibid., 25.

23. Ibid., 31.

24. Ibid., 30.

25. Ibid., 42–48.

26. Quoted in Darrell L. Bock, *Breaking the Da Vinci Code* (Nashville: Thomas Nelson, 2004), 119–20.

27. Hill, *Who Chose the Gospels?* 41.

28. *Against Heresies* 3.1.1, Edward Rochie Hardy, trans., in *Early Christian Fathers*, ed. Cyril Richardson (New York: Touchstone, 1996), 370.

29. Hill, *Who Chose the Gospels?* 37.

30. "The Gospel of Thomas," trans. Thomas O. Lambdin, in *The Nag Hammadi Library in English*, rev. ed., ed. James M. Robinson (San Francisco: HarperSanFrancisco, 1990), 138.

31. Craig A. Evans, *Luke*, New International Biblical Commentary (Peabody, MA: Hendrickson, 1990), 17.

32. I. Howard Marshall, *The Gospel of Luke,* The New International Greek Testament Commentary (Grand Rapids: Eerdmans, 1978), 39; Evans, *Luke*, 17–18.

33. Darrell L. Bock, *Luke 1:1–9:50,* Baker Exegetical Commentary on the New Testament (Grand Rapids: Baker Academic, 1994), 54.

34. Ibid., 55.

35. Ibid., 56.

36. Ibid., 53.

37. Ibid., 58.

38. Marshall, *Luke*, 42.

39. Bock, *Luke 1:1–9:50*, 61. Bock bases his decision on the parallel between *anōthen* ("from the beginning" or "a long time" and the expression *ap' archēs* ("from the first" or "from the beginning") in both Luke 1:2–3 and Acts 26:4–5.

40. *Against Heresies* 3.11.18 in *Early Christian Fathers*, 382.

Conclusion

1. A. Catherine Hankey, "I Love to Tell the Story."